THE GUIDE TO GOOD GRADES

LOUISE and DOUG
COLLIGAN

SCHOLASTIC BOOK SERVICES
New York Toronto London Auckland Sydney Tokyo

To my former students . . .
they were always A+ in my book.

"Mizz Colligan"

ISBN: 0-590-30001-6

20 19 18 17 16 15 14 13 12 11 10 9   3 4 5 6 7/8

Printed in the U.S.A.   01

CONTENTS

Chapter 3. ON ASSIGNMENT: STUDYING AND DOING HOMEWORK

Chapter 6. CHECK IT OUT: SCHOOL SURVIVAL CHECKLISTS AND FORMS

Chapter 1

GET IT TOGETHER: A Plan for Making the Grade in School

If you've been coasting along on grades that just miss the mark, this book will show you how just a little more organization, time, and effort will help you make the grades you want. Usually the difference between one grade and a higher one isn't from extra brain cells or a high I.Q., but is the result of using time and energy more efficiently.

You may have different reasons for reading this book. Maybe last year you would have gotten a B in English instead of a C+ if you had just spent one more day on that big term paper. Or you may have missed out on a decent grade in biology because you told your teacher once too often that your dog ate your homework. Or perhaps that D in history would have been a C if you had had readable class notes instead of cartoons on the pages where your notes on the Boston Tea Party should have been.

So whether you're winging your way through school on less than terrific grades, or aceing your courses but wearing yourself out, this book will show you how to get more out of school in the most effective ways possible.

IT'S ALL IN YOUR HEAD: HOW TO DEVELOP A POSITIVE ATTITUDE ABOUT SCHOOL

Somewhere on most report cards is a space marked "Attitude." "Attitude" is one of those loaded words many students dread hearing, particularly from teachers whose classes they would like to avoid. What is attitude anyway? Why is it so important? And where can you get some fast? If all you want to do is get through chemistry without flunking, then what does your attitude have to do with it anyway?

Many students defeat themselves in school by thinking: "I hate my classes. I'm going to flunk. What's the point? I can't stand my teachers; they can't stand me. Maybe I'll just sit in back all year and hope no one notices me." Does that sound like anything you've thought before? If so, then maybe a losing attitude is getting in your way. What can you do about it?

Use the early advantages you have at the beginning of the semester. Unless you have a bad press agent or got caught throwing water balloons in the teachers' lounge last year, you and everyone else begin new classes on the same footing. On the first day of school, your teachers have no way of knowing you're no Albert Einstein or can't remember when to double consonants. Don't let your teachers find out! Keep them guessing as long as possible.

Teachers form impressions of you from things other than exams, homework, or papers. If you slink into class like a wounded animal, or mumble responses as though you're afraid of your own voice, they are going to get an impression that may have little to do with your actual abilities.

What's the solution? While you've got an edge, take advantage of it. Look alive and prepared when you come to class. If you have a choice of seats, sit where the teacher can see you. Even if you don't feel totally confident, try to fake it for a while. Maybe after psyching yourself like this for a few weeks, you'll start to believe in yourself.

END ZONE: HOW TO SET REASONABLE GOALS FOR YOURSELF

The subject of setting goals could almost be a book in itself, but we'll keep it simple. Giving yourself something to shoot for is the first step toward getting yourself together in school. Here are some problems students often have in setting realistic goals. Look them over and see if you can adapt some of the solutions to your own situation:

1. You don't have any particular goals for yourself. If that problem describes you, then you're like a driver who sets out on a trip without knowing your destination. You'll end up somewhere —maybe even where you want to go—but you'll waste a lot of time getting there.

At the beginning of the school year, try to think of one small thing you would like to accomplish, or a small bad habit you would like to break. For example, if your only solution to a boring class is clock watching, see if you can go at least a half hour without looking at it. If you always seem to be without a pen or pencil, make it a goal to have one every day for a week. If you're an incurable whisperer, see if you can go through an entire period without talking to your friend in the next seat. Although these may seem like small things to work for, setting a few simple goals is a good goal in itself.

2. Your goals are too high, so you give up after the first setback. Are you the kind of student who starts out great guns every year, then falls apart when the first quiz comes back with a B instead of an A? That's like the chronic dieter who starves for days, then goes on an eating binge after one bite of a potato chip. Schoolwork doesn't have to be an all-or-nothing balancing act. Put things in perspective. If languages have always been difficult for you, don't expect to be at the top of your Spanish class. Shooting for a good solid B is better than throwing in the towel just because you didn't ace that first quiz.

3. *Your goals are too low.* Maybe math problems are really a breeze for you, so you don't do much in the course. This is fine if you're at the top of the class in your easiest subject. If not, set higher standards for yourself. If the work is too easy, make arrangements with your teacher or counselor for more advanced work in that subject. When you're good at something, it's important to raise your expectations or you'll wind up disgusted with yourself at the end of the semester.

4. *You are trying to meet someone else's goals instead of your own.* Sometimes parents expect too much. If you have a parent who expects more than you can reasonably deliver, try to work out realistic goals you both can live with.

First ask yourself if the goal they've set for you is what you want. If it is, ask yourself if you really have the talent, skills, and the time to reach it. For example, if your father expects you to be a math whiz and you want that too, then work for it. If that isn't realistic, sit down and discuss what you reasonably expect to achieve. Letting your parents know early in the semester what you plan to work for may prevent a year-end confrontation if you do fall short of reaching their goals. Ask your parents what they expect, listen to their advice, share your own expectations and anxieties, and see if you can work out a compromise early in your courses.

What happens if your parents don't buy this plan? Then you have to try to reach your own goals and satisfy yourself.

A PLACE FOR EVERYTHING: HOW TO GET YOURSELF ORGANIZED AT HOME AND SCHOOL

Organizing schoolwork would be a breeze for some students if they only knew where to find their bus passes in the morning. Very often it's the small details of daily life that slow you down. If you think you are suffering from a chronic case of disorganization, check the following symptoms to diagnose your case:

• You never hear your alarm in the morning (or it takes a near explosion to wake you up).

• You are always missing at least one important piece of clothing five minutes before you're supposed to leave the house.

• You barely make it to your first class (or worse—your first-period teacher has given you up for dead).

- Your locker (or bedroom closet) would be condemned by the Board of Health.
- Your notebook (when you can find it) looks as though a truck ran over it.
- You borrow pens and pencils the way others bum sticks of gum.
- You never write anything down, or, if you do, the scraps of paper you call notes are doomed to become lint in the pockets of your jeans.
- Your idea of breakfast is eating a candy bar while you are struggling to get into your jacket.
- Most of your school assignments are regularly last-minute, panic-button situations.
- You want to get yourself together but don't know where to begin.

You can begin anywhere; just don't try to change your entire life in one day. Make a mental or written list of the small things that keep messing you up—your chaotic locker or closet, your disastrous notebook, or the desk drawers you've been using as a wastebasket for the last five years. Then tackle each problem area one by one. Some suggestions for getting yourself together at home and school:

Your room is your castle and your office. Every working person—and that includes you—needs a base of operations, if only to have a place to throw dirty socks. You have to have somewhere to hang your hat (or bookbag, sneakers, or rock posters). A corner where you can punch a pillow in private is vital to your sanity. And you need space to keep all the things we tell you to get for school later in this chapter. For some disorganized people, even a football stadium wouldn't be big enough. For those who get organized, half a room shared with two gerbils and a kid brother can be enough space.

Most study books suggest that the best study arrangement is a good desk and chair (usually a miserable-looking straight-backed chair a contortionist couldn't get comfortable in) and a good reading lamp with the light beaming over your shoulder (don't ask us why). If that's what's comfortable for you, great. You can make a terrific desk from almost anything: a slab of wood held up by cinder blocks, orange crates, or two-drawer file cabinets. Discount stores and five-and-dimes sell decent lamps that will throw the spotlight on your latest algebra assignment

(which you might prefer to hide under a rock where it could collect moss instead of red pencil marks). If you are the desk-sitting type, find a corner in your house to set up shop.

Some people do their most creative thinking in places other than a straight chair positioned in front of an orderly desk. Maybe the only time you can switch on your gray matter is when you're sitting on the floor, curled up in a chair, or sprawled across your bed.

A floor can be a comfortable study space if you have something soft to sit on—a thick pile rug, a couple of fat pillows, or a foam wedgie to lean against. Add a small table or cube, position a lamp on it, use a length of wooden shelving (or a big flat tray) as a writing surface, and you could run IBM from your floor office.

If your grandfather's old stuffed chair is your favorite place, then it's probably a good study spot too. To turn your chair into a mini-office, just get a length of shelving and lay it over the armrests of the chair. A floor lamp on one side and a small table, bookcase, or plastic cube on the other would give you a study spot to suit your style.

Mark Twain did it, and so can you. What's that? Working in bed. This may sound outrageous, but it is possible to turn your bed into a workable study area. If your parents don't object or mind that the expensive desk they gave you isn't going to get much use, then by all means use your bed as a base of operations.

Again, get yourself a length of shelving (or one of those breakfast trays on legs) to use as a knee-top desk. Prop yourself against your pillows, a wedgie, or a bedrest, and you can use your parents' desk to store your comic-book collection. Don't forget a good lamp and bedside table (after all, where are you going to put down those brownies that are shedding crumbs all over the sheets and your latest masterpiece for English class?).

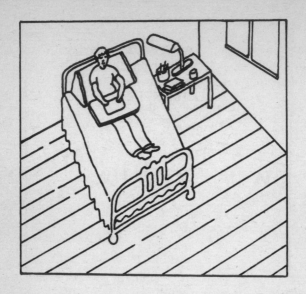

If you have a mobile work space, you need something portable to hold the pencils, scrap paper, dictionary, and other study tools you'll require. Stick all this stuff in a big basket, cube, or tote bag and carry it to your special spot.

If this advice about study space seems casual, it's only because it's not worth getting hung up on where you study as long as the arrangement works for you. When and how you study is far more important than where, as you'll see in Chapter 3. For too many students, homework is unpleasant because they can't seem to get comfortable. Where do you go when you want to curl up with a favorite book or magazine? Go to that same place with your homework. Maybe you'll be more relaxed working there.

One last piece of advice. There's no law that says you have to do homework at home. If screaming brothers and sisters, a blaring TV, or the temptations of your stereo make working at home impossible, then take advantage of your free periods in school to get to a study hall or the library.

TOOLS OF THE TRADE: HOW TO EQUIP YOURSELF FOR SCHOOL

Would you hire a repair person to fix your priceless stereo if he or she showed up without impressive-looking tools? Every job, including yours, has its professional accoutrements (one of which is a dictionary where you can look up that word). There are a few basics which will improve your school life in dozens of big and small ways. Some require a small outlay of money — others just a little common sense. Try to stock up on everything early in the year so you can begin your job feeling confident and well equipped. Here's a list of items no student should be without:

1. Two or three copies of your class schedule — Get one for your notebook, one for your locker, and one for home.

2. A three-ring notebook with clearly labeled dividers for each of your subjects — The notebook can be one of those canvas and pressboard types that will take you right through college, or simply an inexpensive, lightweight plastic kind. (In-

13

evitably at least one teacher will require you to get some off-the-wall special notebook for a particular class. Get it, then carry it around inside the three-ring notebook with the rest of your stuff.) The important thing is to have all your notes and class materials in one place.

3. *An assignment pad* — Pick up a small Monday-Friday homework pad and clip it inside your three-ring notebook. Why a notebook and a pad? Simply because it's hard to keep track of assignments floating around five different sections of your big notebook.

4. *A big supply of notebook paper* — Early in the year, invest in a big package of notebook paper. Keep half at home and half in your locker. That way if you forget your notebook, you'll still have the right-sized paper for your class notes.

5. *A large supply of pens and pencils* — Again, keep some in a jar at home and a bunch in your locker. Your locker stash of school supplies will carry you through those days when you've forgotten everything at home and don't want to go to class empty-handed.

6. *A dictionary* — A good paperback edition is fine unless your teachers ask you to use some other kind.

7. *A thesaurus* — This is an invaluable reference tool that will come in handy when you need five different ways to say a word.

8. *The phone number of one student in each of your classes* — As soon as you have a nodding acquaintance with someone in class, exchange phone numbers so that you can count on each other for notes, homework, and other class in-

formation in case one of you is absent.

9. *A library card* — This is a must. Even if you never plan to set foot in your local library, you can still use the card for identification. More importantly, suppose you don't have a book for Monday's book report? School is closed, and no one at home has anything you want to read. You'll have your library card on hand for your emergency check-out of *Gone With the Wind* (which is where you'll be if you don't get that report done). Get the card even if you hate libraries. When you go to apply for it, you may discover your library carries copies of *Road and Track* magazine going back five years, along with the pilot issues of *Amazing Fiction* or *MAD* magazine.

10. *A wristwatch* — How are you going to know how long it is until lunch unless you can check your watch every nine seconds? You can pick up a decent watch very cheaply. Better yet, ask for one for your next birthday.

The next few items are not absolutely essential to your school survival but can make school life easier for you.

11. *An alarm clock or clock radio* — If your parents have been an unpaid wake-up service for you all these years, it's time to send them into retirement. Better to have three alarm clocks set five minutes apart than be dependent on old Mom and Dad to do the job. Or maybe waking up to the sound of your favorite station on a clock radio would start off your day better. If getting out of bed is a real problem for you, try going to sleep 10 or 15 minutes earlier at night.

12. *A bookbag, knapsack, or tote bag* — These are useful for carrying around life's essentials — from your zoology text to your old gym socks.

13. *A cassette tape recorder* — Believe it or not, this expensive but pleasurable item has a number of uses besides making your favorite sounds available. If you are lucky enough to own one, you can use it to memorize spelling words, vocabulary lists, foreign language idioms, and so on. A tape recorder makes it possible for you to test yourself in a number of areas. For a spelling test, say the words into the recorder, play back the tape, then write down the words. Or read vocabulary definitions into a tape — then play it back until you can "hear" the meanings in your head.

14. *Earplugs* — This is one of those little emergency items that may prevent you from going bananas listening to your sister's endless phone conversations or your upstairs neighbor practicing gymnastics while you are trying to work out algebra equations. You can get them at almost any drugstore.

15. *Pocket calendar, wall calendar, or bulletin board* — Most working people have a system for keeping track of business and social appointments. Again, it's time to retire Mom and Dad if they've been keeping track of babysitting, lawn mowing, or orthodontist appointments for you. Get in the habit of writing everything down — from your dog-walking job on Saturday morning to the shoes you have to drop off at the shoemaker's tomorrow afternoon.

IT'S ABOUT TIME: SET UP A WORKABLE SCHOOL SCHEDULE

One reason many students hate the idea of making up schedules for themselves is because most don't allow for things like staring into the mirror for hours on end, picking lint off your sweater as you daydream about next Saturday night, or looking out the window at nothing in particular. Scheduling schoolwork makes a lot more sense if you give yourself plenty of time for these things.

Being on schedule doesn't mean punching a time clock every day. Nor does it mean carrying around a card telling you what you're supposed to be doing every minute of the day. After all, you see very few adults running around with charts and timetables. Most working people use small pocket calendars or wall or desk calendars to keep track of specific appointments or deadlines. The rest of their day's schedule is in their heads.

You already have a class schedule which accounts for your time in school. Here's a chart to help you figure out how to spend the rest of your time. Once you complete it, you probably won't have to look at it again. Just the process of knowing where and how you spend your time is the first step in learning to control it. And remember, if you fill out the chart, leave yourself a few spaces for those special, private times.

ON TIME

	Sun.	Mon.	Tues.	Wed.	Thurs.	Fri.	Sat.
9:00							
10:00							
11:00							
12:00							
1:00							
2:00							
3:00							
4:00							
5:00							
6:00							
7:00							
8:00							
9:00							
10:00							
11:00							

Suppose you have accounted for your time on the preceding schedule. You have listed your part-time job; you've allowed time for studying, eating, sleeping, and spending leisure time. Terrific. The only problem is that you need a 33-hour day instead of the usual 24. Your next step is to figure out how to use the time you have more efficiently. Listed below are some time-draining activities and ways to cope with them. We've also added a few suggestions on how to do certain things at the same time. Here goes:

1. *Lay out your clothes, books, keys, wallet, bus money or pass in the same place every school night.* That way when you're bleary-eyed and running late the next day, you'll know where everything is without having to hunt around frantically.

2. *Don't let television run your life.* Most people have those evenings when they sit down to watch a half-hour show, only to find themselves three hours later bug-eyed in front of some ridiculous program they had no intention of watching. If you get *TV Guide* or some other weekly listing in your house, look it over when it arrives. Circle all the programs you plan to watch during that week. Then don't watch anything you haven't circled. If you know you have to see that first-run showing of a favorite movie, then do your homework in the afternoon so you'll have the evening free for the movie. If Tuesday is a dead night on the tube, get ahead on your weekly assignments that evening to give yourself more free time later in the week.

3. *Learn how to hang up the phone.* This not only prevents cauliflower ear, it gives you more

time for doing other things. Next to television, the telephone offers more distractions per minute than any other modern invention. Your history teacher probably won't consider a two-hour phone call an acceptable substitute for a completed assignment. So what do you do when the phone rings and you're in the middle of reading about the Napoleonic Wars? Just say: "Can I call you back in half an hour?" No need for an explanation. It's also not a bad idea to work out general calling times with your friends — times when you both know you can talk without having the next day's history quiz on the brain.

4. *Bribe yourself with pleasurable activities.* Just knowing a favorite book or record is waiting when you finish your math problems may be just the boost you need to get through the work.

5. *Make use of small blocks of time.* While you watch television or listen to your stereo, you can exercise, file your nails, clean out your notebook, iron your jeans, rewrite your class schedule, look up a new word in the dictionary, repot a plant, lift weights, organize your record collection, sew on a missing button, or do a crossword puzzle. There's no law that says you must lie half-comatose while watching TV or listening to music. You can do certain things at the same time. Just one word of warning. Albert Einstein did not work out the theory of relativity while talking on the phone, catching reruns on the tube, or listening to the Rolling Stones. Nor can you do your assignments justice if your mind is on one thing and your eyes and ears are someplace else.

SCHOOL PROBLEMS: HOW TO COPE WITH SCHOOL HANG-UPS

Even A+ students sometimes have problems dealing with difficult teachers, demanding schedules, boring classes, distracting friends, or overly concerned parents. Any one of these situations can make you feel like burying yourself under the covers for the rest of the school year. Fortunately, there are a number of constructive ways to deal with these problems. Here are a few:

1. Problem teachers or classes —Somewhere in the laws of chance is a rule which states that for all the terrific teachers you get, you'll get at least one who set out to become a drill sergeant but switched to teaching instead. How do you handle a tough class?

a. First of all, try to let your good teachers set the tone for your day instead of letting a bad one ruin it.

b. Always be completely prepared, prompt, and alert in a problem class. Preventive measures lessen the possibilities of a conflict.

c. If you are the object of a teacher's anger or sarcasm, try counting the nails in the floor instead of blowing up. If you decide a situation warrants it and your pride is really on the line, see if you can figure out a way to save yourself without setting off a public explosion. Maybe you'll have to back down during class and talk to your teacher later in the day when each of you has cooled off. Although it's your teacher's job to find a way out of a confrontation, maybe you're better at cooling down a hot situation.

d. If you have a running battle with a teacher, go to a teacher or counselor whom you like and respect for suggestions on how to handle the problem.

e. Think about whether there's something you might be doing that ticks off your teacher. Are you always hacking around with the class wits in the back of the room? Are you unprepared more often than not? Are you visibly yawning, sleeping, or otherwise goofing off in class? If so, straighten out your act instead of having your teacher nag you about it.

f. Don't lose sleep over someone you can't change. Remember, that difficult teacher will probably still be teaching the same old class long after you've moved on to other things.

2. *Difficult subjects* — The easiest way of dealing with a hard subject is to throw the textbook for that class under your bed and hope it disappears by morning. Unfortunately, problems with a particular subject don't disappear that simply.

The truth is that you have to devote much more time to a troublesome subject than to one that comes easily to you. It's tempting to avoid a subject that ties your brain in knots, but you'll only get yourself in a deeper hole by pushing it away. Here are some solutions to consider:

a. Spend twice as much time on your problem subjects as the easy ones.

b. Get as much information as possible from your classes.

c. Always ask questions about any material you don't understand in class.

d. Make sure you write down your assignments word for word.

e. Do all your homework in a difficult subject before you tackle other assignments.

f. See if you can find another student in class whom you can call or check with when you're stuck on an assignment.

g. Never skip a class, a test, or an assignment in a difficult class.

h. Always read over your tests, exams, and papers carefully in a difficult subject. Save all of them for future reference. If you don't understand where you went wrong on a test or paper, ask your teacher to go over it with you.

i. Think about getting a tutor in the subject to help you get over hurdles along the way. Or form a study group with two or three other students to tackle the subject in a systematic way.

j. Maintain a positive relationship with your teacher. Most teachers are sympathetic to a student who is making a visible effort to succeed in a tough subject.

k. Students sometimes find themselves in hot water because they didn't catch on to a critical point or step along the way in their course. If this happens, try to backtrack to the point at which you derailed and get help on that particular area.

l. Finally, if you are really in bad shape in

the beginning level of any subject, it's better to get a tutor, go to summer school, or possibly repeat the course than settle for a D and risk having future difficulties in that area. Someday you may decide to become an engineer instead of a painter and you'll need to know your square roots just to be considered for graduate school.

3. *Chronic lateness*—As we mentioned earlier, use a watch, some kind of calendar, and a schedule to keep track of your time and appointments. Pinpoint when and where your latenesses crop up. Are you always late for school? If so, set your alarm early enough, and get your clothes, books, money, and other materials lined up the night before. Keep pushing back your alarm in 10-minute segments until you are running on time in the morning. If being late for classes is the problem, get all the materials from your locker at the beginning of the day so you don't have to keep shuttling back and forth to your locker between classes. Save between-class social breaks for lunchtime or free periods. Try to develop a reputation as a punctual person. That way, if you are unavoidably late once or twice, your teacher will understand.

4. *Missing homework* — Most teachers are pretty fair about bending the rules for students who forget their homework once or twice, but again, it's important to establish your reputation as a student who is usually prepared. If you do happen to miss an assignment, you can work something out with your teacher to bring it in the next day. Keep in mind that teachers usually sit

down with a pile of papers from a single class and evaluate the whole group at once. Accepting late papers throws a monkey wrench into the system, so teachers are often reluctant to accept late work. If you agree to a deadline, do everything you can to meet it.

Above all, stick to your word. Don't worm your way out of a school problem with empty excuses or promises. Even the most patient, good-natured teachers lose faith in students who keep breaking their word. Stick to your commitments. And learn how to express the thought: "Sorry for the inconvenience. It won't happen again."

5. *Poor grades on a test or assignment* — The usual first reaction a student has when he or she receives a lousy grade is to bury the paper face down at the bottom of the wastebasket. While it's a great way to vent frustration, throwing away exams or papers is self-defeating. Start up a file for all your old papers and tests. Make sure you go over all your tests to see where you went right and where you went wrong. Go over compositions to see where certain mistakes keep cropping up. This is really the only way to determine your strengths and weaknesses. If you don't understand why you got a particular grade on a test or paper, see your teacher quietly after class. Don't cry: "Foul!" or "Unfair!" Simply ask your teacher to go over the test with you because you want to know where you went wrong. With some teachers, it may even be possible to do an extra-credit assignment to counterbalance a really low grade. Suggest this if you feel your

teacher might be receptive. If not, try to learn from your test and hope for better next time around.

6. *Bad report card*—Students who come home with disastrous grades usually have had some advance warnings along the way. A poor final grade is generally the result of a series of problems which have been building up for a while. In the face of a poor report, you can soften the blow to your parents in a number of ways. First, prepare them for the shock ahead of time. Let them know when you are having difficulties in a subject during the semester. Second, have a plan of attack. Let them know how seriously you've been thinking about your school problems and how you plan to remedy the situation next semester.

WITH FRIENDS LIKE THAT...HOW TO MAKE SURE YOUR FRIENDS ARE ON YOUR SIDE

Who needs friends who are always getting good grades anyway? Every student who's miserable with mediocre grades, that's who. While it's comforting to have a down-and-out friend with whom you can share your misery, it's better to enjoy success with another person who has also done well in a tough course. The point is that friends can sometimes make it hard for you to get tough on yourself.

If your friends think goofing off is more cool than school, it may be time to put them to the test — and not an algebra or botany test either. The test is this: Will your friends stick by you if you say you have to study Wednesday night instead of spending another exciting evening watching people park cars down at the shopping mall? Will your best friend feel insulted if you tell her you can only talk for five minutes because you have to get back to your French verbs? Will your buddies stop snickering if you get up in front of class and work out a tricky math problem? Can you still be friends if you start doing well in school and your old cronies are still just squeaking through?

These are hard questions. Birds of a feather usually enjoy each other's company, and if you fly off in another direction, you may, in fact, jeopardize your relationship with old friends who are stuck in a rut. What can you do about it?

First of all, a true-blue friend will stick by you no matter what. Maybe there's a way you can move ahead together. Sometimes it just takes one person to lead the way. Stop downgrading school with your friends. You don't have to become a public-relations person for school, but avoid contributing to negative or self-defeating attitudes your friends may have about school. If you suddenly start moving ahead in school, don't lord it over your buddies. See if you can expand your circle of friends to include one or two people who happen to be fun and smart in school. Finally, it is possible to stay friends with people who aren't necessarily academic types.

Just make sure that while they do their non-school thing you can do your special thing too. This means that good friends will understand what you are up to without making you feel uncomfortable about it.

Chapter 2

A CLASS ACT: Getting the Most From Your Classes

ROLL CALL: SHOW UP FOR ALL YOUR CLASSES

Woody Allen once gave an anxious friend a T-shirt inscribed: "Most of life is just showing up." Not a bad piece of advice to keep in mind on those days when you are tempted to cut a class or stay home watching soap operas.

Even if you just pick up information in class by osmosis (the passing of a substance through a semi-permeable membrane, unofficially known as learning while you daydream), your appearance in class is preferable to the presence of cuts or absences on your report card. When you skip classes, you miss out on important announcements, lessons, and other information essential to your job as a student.

FIRST, SECOND, AND THIRD CLASS: HOW TO ADJUST YOURSELF TO THE DEMANDS OF DIFFERENT CLASSES

Another basic requirement for doing well in school is figuring out what you are supposed to get from each of your courses. Your teachers have unique styles, methods, and objectives to their classes. Let's take a look at different types of classes.

1. *The discussion class* — In this kind of class, the teacher expects you to learn by participating and interacting with other students. This doesn't mean your discussions should turn into long-winded sessions or shouting matches. A good teacher knows how to structure a discussion that is meaningful, stimulating, and informative. In this kind of class, your teacher's role is to keep things running smoothly and see that no one monopolizes the conversation. Your job is to stay involved in the discussion and speak up when it's appropriate. Many potentially interesting discussions fall flat because each student decides to let the next guy speak. Don't be afraid to be the first person to get the ball rolling.

To do justice to a discussion class, you have to be familiar with the assigned material when you come in. This means that as you read over the homework, you should give some thought to what questions and topics might come up in class. In a discussion, knowing facts isn't as important as understanding ideas.

Note-taking is helpful, but it is not the most basic part of this kind of class. Keep your notebook handy in case there are major discussion points your teacher wants you to note. Examples of how to take notes in a discussion class are shown on page 51.

2. *The lecture class* — As you move up through the higher grades, you will be taking more and more lecture classes. In college, most of your classes will be conducted as lectures. In this kind of class, the teacher usually has a lot of information she wants you to know and has a fairly structured way of presenting it.

Because a lecture class doesn't require your active verbal input, this kind of class affords more opportunities for snoozing, daydreaming, or doodling. Don't fall into the trap! It's vital to participate as an active listener and note-taker in a lecture class. Note-taking is extremely important here, so pay plenty of attention to the sections in this chapter on writing good notes. Examples of poor and good lecture notes are shown on pages 49-50.

3. *The lab class* — This is usually considered a foreign language or science class, but we use the term to describe any class in which students are expected to work actively on a project. This can mean solving math problems during the period, writing a first draft of a paper in class, dissecting a frog in biology, painting a canvas in art, or practicing jump shots in gym. A lab is often the

most enjoyable of all classes since it involves physical activity.

With the exception of science labs, note-taking in a lab class usually isn't as important as it is in other types of classes. Again, though, you and your teacher have to determine when it's important to take down notes, so keep your notebook and pen nearby.

4. *The combination class* — Most of your classes in junior high and high school will be a mix of the three types. On some days, your teacher may want to deliver a straight lecture with little feedback or discussion from the class. On those days, be especially prepared to take good notes. On other days, your teacher may want you to work on writing, problem solving, conducting experiments, and so forth. Have your notebook ready, and particularly get yourself in gear for active work on the subject. If your teacher begins a class like this, "Today we're going to talk about...", chances are the class will be conducted as a discussion. You'll have to adjust your note-taking to the kind of material presented. Usually your teacher will point out what you should write down.

What all these classes have in common is the requirement that you participate in some way. Sure, your teacher is the one who's being paid to get up there and perform. However, if you think about any skill you've ever learned, you know that one important part of the learning was doing. For example, you can read about how to make a paper airplane or watch someone demonstrate its construction, but until you actually build and fly one of your own, you won't learn much about aerodynamics. In order to pick up any skill, you have to be involved in some way. Keep that in mind the next time your teacher asks you to conjugate a verb, answer a question, work out a theorum, or take notes in class.

SPEAK OUT: HOW TO PARTICIPATE IN CLASS INTELLIGENTLY

Being active in class doesn't mean you have to turn into one of those students who is always trying to score points. Most teachers get just as bored as you do with the inevitable student in every class who always monopolizes class time with perfect answers delivered in a know-it-all voice. That's not what class participation means.

Every teacher appreciates a student who makes an honest attempt to share ideas, insights, opinions, or even doubts about a subject without having to be a star. Participating in class intelligently means arriving prepared to get involved in the work. If you know the answer to a question, and can support your opinion when called upon, then by all means feel free to speak up confidently.

If you don't know an answer when your teacher calls on you, be honest and say you don't know. Just a simple, "I'm sorry, but I couldn't figure that out when I read it," is satisfactory. If you're not prepared and know nothing about the topic at hand, you're better off facing the consequences than faking it and having your teacher publicly confront you with your lack of preparation. In the face of such a possibility, just say: "Sorry, I'm not prepared today. I'll look it up tonight." Then follow through. Keep in mind, though, that few teachers will buy that statement often. Don't abuse a teacher's goodwill by constantly serving up phony excuses instead of real answers.

WHO, WHAT, WHEN, WHERE, WHY: HOW TO ASK INTELLIGENT QUESTIONS

Sometimes the ball is in your court and you are in the position of needing an answer instead of providing one. Asking questions is an important part of a student's job, and answering them is a major part of your teacher's role in helping you learn.

If you've been conscientious about doing your outside work and listening in class, there's no such thing as a stupid question. Teachers make mistakes, textbooks are not always clear, and directions are sometimes confusing. You can bet if you're thinking about asking a seemingly stupid question, there are one or two other intelligent students who would like to know the same thing. So ask away. Simply raise your hand and say, "Can you explain such and such?" Or, "I'm a little confused about that last point. Can you explain it in another way?" Sometimes an idea is confusing until your teacher provides a few examples that illustrate the point. When this is the case, just ask, "Could you give us an example of how that works?" Teachers need feedback in the form of student questions to keep a discussion on target, so don't be afraid to speak up.

If your question is really involved or seems so elementary you're afraid of embarrassing yourself by asking it in class, then make a note of it and discuss it with your teacher after class. If you have a teacher who isn't receptive to student questions, see if a classmate or someone else can help you out. Whatever you do, don't crawl into a shell and hope that somehow your confusion will clear up automatically. Get the problem straightened out when it arises.

JUST SHY: COPING WITH SHYNESS IN CLASS

Suppose the thought of speaking publicly is enough to give you a permanent case of the shakes, but a teacher expects everyone to speak up anyway. How do you conquer your stage fright?

First, be prepared for class. Some people dread speaking up because they don't know enough about the subject to talk about it. Make sure you've done the required outside work for each class. If something is unclear about the material, check it out with your teacher.

Shyness doesn't always stem from lack of preparation. Maybe you do know the answers, but hate the idea of having to say anything while people are watching you. If you can, sit near the front of the room. That way almost everyone else will be behind you and you won't have 25 pairs of eyes riveted on you as you speak. If you usually wait for the teacher to call on you, then take the matter into your own hands occasionally and volunteer to answer questions you know inside out. That way you are controlling the conditions. Just raise your hand, take a deep breath, focus on the teacher, and say what you planned to say. If you volunteer from time to time, you'll lessen the chances of having your teacher call on you when you're nervous about the material.

ATTENTION, ATTENTION: HOW TO COPE WITH DISTRACTIONS IN CLASS

1. *The class clown* — From *Our Miss Brooks* in the 50's, to *Room 222* in the 60's, down to *Happy Days* and *Welcome Back, Kotter* in the 70's, comedy writers have found the classroom a gold mine of humor. The heroes of these shows were generally "dez-dem-and-doz" guys who were long on wisecracks and short on grammar. All those TV writers probably based their characters on the real-life class wits you can find in nearly

every school in the country. Where most of these programs fell down was in showing the class clown pitted against a stodgy, dull-witted teacher who couldn't talk his way out of the principal's office. In real life, good teachers know how to use funny students to advantage. Feel free to enjoy a class in which the teacher can trade punch lines and routines with the class comics, yet still teach the subject effectively.

However, teachers have their own styles and quirks. If every good teacher were a comedian, school officials would be selling tickets to classes instead of worrying about class attendance. Humor doesn't suit every person's style, and nothing is more embarrassing than to watch a basically serious teacher trying to make feeble jokes. You're going to come across teachers who have plenty to offer, even if their delivery doesn't exactly have you falling off your chair. You may discover that a poker-faced teacher can engage your interest in a particular subject without having to make jokes about it. In such a class, it's time to play it straight and let the class clown go it alone. Don't expect a serious teacher to find a replay of someone's last date hilarious while she's trying to teach you how cells divide. If the mood of your teacher and nearly everyone else is quiet, don't be an audience for the class clown. Comedy is funny because it breaks up the day. If it's breaking up the mood of your class, give the comedy routine a rest.

2. *The note passer* — Unless someone in history class is passing you a note on how the Industrial Revolution affected farm labor, let the pas-

ser send her note on to someone else. The greatest temptation for any teacher who intercepts a note is to read the message aloud to the class. Do you really want everyone to hear about the fight you and your boyfriend had last night? If not, then don't pass it on in writing.

3. *The whisperer* — Whisperers are often people who have little to say unless they can speak in dramatic, hushed tones while class is going on. How do you deal with your buddy in the seat behind you who's always whispering vitally important messages in your ear? Just tell him you'll see him after class. Few teachers will tolerate for long the constant disruptions and rudeness of chronic whisperers. Save it for later.

HEAR, HEAR: HOW TO DEVELOP GOOD LISTENING HABITS

Since you've been listening to things all your life without having to learn how from a book, you may be tempted to skip over this and move on to the note-taking section. However, listening and note-taking are two closely related skills, and you will never become an accurate note-taker until you learn to listen in a structured way.

Good listening habits are important for a number of reasons. First, verbal memory — what you hear aloud and register in your mind — is the best reinforcement of material you are trying to learn. Second, you have no way of controlling what a teacher says or how he says it. Good listening helps you make sense out of information that may be presented too quickly, too slowly, or too chaotically. Whether or not you are interested in a class, it moves along with or without your attention. Since you are there, you might as well pick up the information as efficiently as possible. Here are several ways to develop good listening skills:

1. *Read your work before you go to class.* This helps you anticipate what the class is going to be about.

2. *Be on time for class.* It's much harder to follow a speaker if you miss the opening comments and have to fill in the blank spots. Most speakers introduce their main points at the beginning of their talk.

3. *Try to leave your personal problems outside the class.* If you are still stewing about the disagreement you had with a friend, it's going to be a lot harder for you to process information about right angles or root words. When you mull over personal problems in class, you wind up with two problems — the same one you came in with and the problem you're going to have understanding the material. If you really can't shake off a personal problem — and that happens to everyone occasionally — see if you can borrow another student's notes. That way you can at least go over the material later when you're ready for it.

4. *If you can choose your seat in class, sit fairly close to the front of the room.* It's much easier to follow a speech when you can make eye contact with the speaker. Sitting near the front gives you

fewer opportunities for distractions and more chances for hearing and seeing what the teacher is up to.

5. *If you wear glasses or contact lenses, make sure you have them on in class.* Nothing is more headache producing than squinting at the teacher and trying to decipher all those squiggles he's writing on the board.

6. *Be alert to your teacher's opening and closing remarks on a subject.* Most good speakers follow the old politician's advice: "First I tell 'em what I'm goin' to tell 'em; then I tell 'em; and then I tell 'em what I told 'em." Makes sense for any speaker. Good speakers and writers realize the importance of driving home the same point in different ways.

7. *Listen for "buzz" words.* Buzz words are signals speakers use to alert you they are about to make an important point. So pay special attention when you hear any of the following buzz words:

Openers:
"First,... Second,... Third,..."
"A major development..."
"Remember that..."
"Take note of..."
"Notice that..."
"The basic idea is..."
"Now this is important..."
"The reason is this..."

Supporting Material:
"For example..."
"For instance..."
"Furthermore..."
"As an example..."
"Similarly..."
"In contrast..."
"On the other hand..."
"Also..."

Conclusions:
"Finally..."
"In summary..."
"As a result..."
"From this we can see..."
"Therefore..."
"In conclusion..."

8. *Follow your teacher's body language and listen for changes in tone of voice.* Most speakers use their hands, posture, facial expression, and tone of voice to emphasize main ideas.

9. *Form silent questions about the material as your teacher moves along.* Write down any questions you would like to have answered later on.

10. *Reinforce what you hear with good notes.* (The next section in this chapter will show you how.)

11. *If you weren't paying attention in a particular class, get someone else's notes afterward.* Let's face it, everyone has bad days. Getting borrowed notes is a good safety measure on a lousy day.

TAKE NOTE: HOW TO TAKE ORGANIZED CLASS NOTES

Class notes are a real hurdle for many students because they can't decide what to write down. Some students complain, "It's all a big blur to me." Or, "I can't write as fast as the teacher talks." Or, "I never use my notes anyway, so why bother?" Here are some reasons for taking the trouble:

• Note-taking reinforces and coordinates the class material with your outside assignments.

• Notes give you permanent review material for exams and papers.

• Class notes help you identify and focus on key points in your classes.

• Note-taking turns you into an active class participant.

• Notes provide you with a record of any new material that doesn't appear in the outside reading.

• Without notes, you'll probably recall only half of the class material after a week. Good notes will help you remember more than three-quarters of the class information even two weeks later.

As you move up through high school and college, note-taking becomes a bigger part of your job. At the college level, student notes are an absolute essential. Yet despite the importance of class notes, many students never really learn how to take them or how to use them. Here is a

10-step plan for note-taking followed by examples of what good notes look like:

1. *Be prepared for class so you can preview the main points of what the teacher will cover in class.* Base your listening and note-taking on what you've already read.

2. *Date your notes and record the name of the class on the sheet of paper.* Leave at least a half dozen lines between each day's set of notes.

3. *Leave wide margins on each sheet for personal notes to yourself.*

4. *Record only the main ideas a teacher emphasizes.* The first time a teacher asks students to take class notes, often their first temptation is to write down everything. The purpose of note-taking is to help you focus on main points; otherwise, you might as well send a tape recorder to class in your place. To help you determine what to write down, here's a quick replay of what to listen for:

   a. *Pay close attention to opening and closing comments.*

   b. *Listen for "buzz" words.*

   c. *Write down any idea your teacher keeps repeating.*

   d. *Watch for gestures and listen for changes in your teacher's tone of voice.*

   e. *Take notes on any material your teacher writes on the board.* Always copy diagrams, charts, or graphs from the board. Teachers generally don't go to the trouble of writing things out unless they consider the information important.

5. *Restate and summarize your teacher's main*

ideas in the fewest possible words. Don't try to write down every word — just those which clearly convey the idea. Explain these ideas in your own words. This helps you think about what the statements really mean.

6. *Arrange main ideas under headings*. You can do this in outline form or according to a workable system you develop yourself. We'll show you examples of how to do this.

7. *If you have time, write down at least one example under your main idea headings*. Teachers provide examples to show you how an idea works. When you read your notes later on, one or two specific examples will refresh your memory of the main point.

8. *Call attention to important words with your own personal symbols*. Use boxes, capital letters, underlinings, circles, stars, dots, question marks, or exclamation points to highlight really major points. Here are a few examples:

<u>underline</u>   box

circle   ★ star ★

PUT IN CAPS

9. Use abbreviations or other shorthand symbols only if you understand them. Listed below are a few shorthand symbols you might want to work into your notes. Again, make sure you'll understand what they mean later on; otherwise you may wind up wondering if you took your notes in Chinese.

+	plus	i.e.	for example
−	minus	w/	with
=	equal	w/o	without
>	greater than	∴	therefore
<	less than	info	information
re	regarding, referring to	avg	average

10. Always get someone else's notes if you missed a class or took messy or unreadable notes during a particular period.

You're probably a better note-taker than you think. Taking notes is similar to making lists. You listen to detailed information; you process it in your head; then you boil everything down to a few key words or phrases that will ring a bell when you reread them. We've already described how to listen for main ideas. Once you master that step, you're on your way to becoming a good note-taker.

Here's an example of how a detailed set of everyday directions can be reduced to an easy-to-follow list:

"Could you go down to the shopping center and pick up a few things? First, stop by the drugstore and pick up my prescription. It's already paid for. While you're there, get two radio batteries and an eight-ounce bottle of rubbing alcohol — store brand. Oh yes, stop by the photo counter at the drugstore and pick up my pictures. They've already been paid for too. I could also use another roll of color-slide film — 36 exposures. On second thought, get the film at Lampert's; they're having a sale, and it's right next door to the drugstore. By the time you're out of there, my boots should be ready. The shoemaker said 4:30. Thanks, you're a lifesaver. Oh, and on the way home, fill the tank with unleaded. It's on me. Here's the money for everything.''

This involved set of instructions can be reduced to this simple list:

> *drugstore:*
> prescription (paid for)
> 2 radio batteries
> rubbing alcohol (8 oz. store brand)
>
> *Lampert's*
> color-slide film (36 ex.)
>
> *shoemaker's:*
> boots (aft. 4:30)
>
> *gas station:*
> unleaded

While the content of information you get in class may be different, the note-taking system is basically the same as one you would use to write up a list of errands. In some ways, it's like composing a telegram. You get the message across in the fewest possible words. This means using phrases and single words instead of complete sentences.

Following is an excerpt of a social studies lecture on student rights. Examples of poor notes and organized notes based on this excerpt are shown on the following pages.

Class Lecture:

"Today I would like to discuss the question of student rights and responsibilities. One of the most important early cases in the United States was *Hill vs. Dickinson College* in 1886. This particular case was unusual because it upheld a student's individual right to due process over the right of an educational institution to dismiss a student without a hearing. This case involved a student, John Hill, who claimed he was unfairly expelled from Dickinson College without proper notification. The college had dismissed Hill for unruly behavior without specifying the dismissal charges and without a proper hearing. Hill brought suit against the college and won his case.

"In contrast, the majority of later cases involving students and schools swung the other way. By the 20's, courts upheld the rights of institutions over those of students. For example, schools during that decade dismissed students for a whole range of reasons without fair hearing.

Failure to conform to a school's image, off-campus smoking or drinking, or student complaints against the faculty were some of the various charges which led to college dismissals. Most of these expulsions took place without any kind of hearing.

"Now the pendulum is swinging the other way. Since the 60's, student rights have noticeably expanded. The trend is toward giving students the civil rights any citizen would have. Significantly, these rights have been granted by the schools themselves and stated in school policies, student bills of rights, special codes, and so on. Many rights have come about from the institutions rather than from the courts. Many educational institutions have promoted the right of any student to gain access to a higher education. Students have also gained rights to fair hearings and freedom of expression.

"Currently, the laws and educational policies are unclear about a student's right to free expression. Students have been expelled for displaying certain kinds of political insignia, failing to salute the flag, refusing to conform to dress codes, or publishing controversial student newspapers. In these areas, there has been considerable legal action yet to be settled. In fact, in the area of a student's right to free expression, there has been more legal action taken than in all other areas of student rights combined.

"In summary, huge numbers of cases now remain to be settled in courts which are ill-equipped to handle the problems. The best way to expand student rights is for students and schools to work together in an orderly fashion to bring about changes."

Poorly Written Notes

Student Rights & Responsibilities

Early U.S. case, *Hill vs. Dickinson College*, 1886, was about a student's right to due process. College dismissed John Hill for bad behavior without hearing. Didn't list charges against Hill. Hill brought suit and won.

Later cases gave more power to schools. In 20's, schools could dismiss students for smoking off campus or not conforming to school image — without hearing.

Since 60's, things are back the other way. Students have more rights — like those citizens have. Rights have been granted by institutions rather than courts. Most important: right to pursue higher education. Others: fair hearing and freedom of expression.

Laws still confused about freedom of student expression. Dismissals for political displays, non-conformity, publishing still being argued; not settled.

Summary: Too many cases before courts which can't handle load. Better for students to organize with schools to expand rights.

These notes attempt to reproduce the entire excerpt. Try to imagine writing in this much detail for 30 or 40 minutes in class. And think about what it would be like to wade through pages and pages of similar notes the night before an exam.

Here is an example of notes from the same lecture. In half the time and half the space, these notes sum up all the main ideas.

Clear, Concise Notes

Topic: Student Rights   American Government
3/17/79

I. Development student rights
  A. Earliest — *Hill vs. Dickinson College*, 1886 — student upheld
    1. Hill dismissed w/o cause
    2. Court reinstates students
  B. 1920's — courts uphold school authorities
    1. No due process
    2. Expulsions w/o hearings
      a. Off-campus smoking, drinking
      b. Non-conformity
  C. Since 60's — students favored again
    1. Many same rights as citizens
    2. Schools developed favorable student rights
II. Rights being tested now — not yet decided
  A. Freedom of expression
    1. political display   ⎫ currently
    2. dress codes   ⎬ most
    3. student newspapers   ⎭ controversial
  B. Summary
    1. Courts can't handle all the cases
    2. Students and schools should organize a way to define and expand rights.

We've used the standard outline form because it's the most organized way to break down information into main ideas, supporting points, and examples. In an outline, you eliminate the need for connecting words. If you prefer, you can adapt the outlining system to your own style. Whatever your system, use main ideas as an umbrella covering supporting points and examples.

This system also comes in handy for outlining textbook chapters, answering essay questions, writing essays, and drafting speeches. As a note-taking style, the outlining method works best in a structured class lecture. For group discussions, try the system shown below. First, divide your notebook page into three columns at the beginning of class. Listen for key points in the discussion. List them in the first column. Write a key word or phrase describing the main idea in the middle column. Add your own comments or your teacher's remarks in the right-hand column.

Statements	Main Ideas	Your comments/ Teacher comments

Once you have good notes, use them. Read them over for test review. Find important information in your notes to emphasize or develop in your written work. Use your notes to clear up confusing sections of your reading. Finally, save all your notes for future reference. At the beginning of a new course, go back to your old notes from the previous year and use them as a bridge from one course level to the next.

Chapter 3

ON ASSIGNMENT: Studying and Doing Homework

On a list of frequently asked student questions, "Why do we have to have homework?" must rank somewhere near the top. And next to, "Because you have to, that's why," some of the most common teacher replies would include the following:

• Homework reinforces the information presented in class.

• Homework is the practice part of learning. Just as you repeat and practice any new skill you want to master — from sports to hobbies — homework provides you with a way of developing academic skills on your own.

• Homework — the exercises, reading, writing, memorizing, and note-taking — is a systematic way of preparing you for class discussions, quizzes, and exams.

• Finally, the process of scheduling, organizing, and doing outside assignments helps you develop your own work habits.

Ideally these are the best reasons teachers have for assigning homework. Undoubtedly you will come across some teachers who seem arbitrary about it. The assignments they give don't necessarily strengthen your skills, help you develop good work habits, or do anything but cause you headaches. While it may be tempting to forget about seemingly pointless assignments, you're stuck with them. See if you can find at least one redeeming thing about each assignment. If you can't, just do them; then move on to subjects that are more challenging.

HOMEWORK BEGINS IN CLASS: HOW TO GET THE ASSIGNMENT AND GET IT RIGHT

Nothing is more frustrating than to sit down ready for work and discover your vocabulary book is back at school and the page numbers of your geometry problems are nowhere to be found.

In the first two chapters of this book, we have stressed the importance of developing good listening, note-taking, and organizing habits. Once you get yourself together in these areas, you greatly lessen the chances of losing books, forgetting assignments, or misunderstanding directions. Here are several additional tips for handling your outside schoolwork effectively:

1. *Don't trust your memory.* Write down all your assignments word for word in your assignment pad. Scraps of paper or little margin notes are out.

2. *Ask your teacher to repeat an assignment or directions if you don't get them all the first time around.*

3. *Underline the due dates or any other information your teacher really stresses about the homework.*

4. *Ask questions about any confusing parts of the assigned material.*

5. *Before you leave class, make sure you understand the purpose of the assignment and what you are expected to get from it.*

6. *Before you leave school for the day, check that you have all the materials you need to bring home for the homework.*

WHAT ARE YOU WAITING FOR: HOW TO STOP PROCRASTINATING

You know the feeling. It goes something like this. On Monday morning your teacher asks you to read and summarize 30 pages in your history textbook by Friday. You go home, toss the book in the corner of your bedroom, go out, check what's on the tube, think about the book for 11 seconds, get up to make a sandwich, go outside and kick pebbles around the backyard, come in, play your new record seven times in a row, look in the mirror, part your hair three different ways, look guiltily at your history book lying in the corner, and finally decide you have lots of time to do the work later in the week.

By Thursday night, you've seen 17 television shows, changed hairstyles 22 times, worn out your new record, and you *still* have 30 pages to read and summarize in your textbook. Finally, around 10:30 the night before the assignment is due, you open the book, realize it's hopeless, and decide to wing it in class the next day.

What's going on here? Just the classic techniques of a master procrastinator. There must be a better way. Procrastination is often a sign of indecision, insecurity, or unrealistic expectations. For example, suppose you decide you have to get an A on your next book report. As long as you keep putting it off, you don't have to face the fact that what you come up with may not be first-rate material. As long as that report stays in your head, it's got great potential. As soon as you get the actual words on paper, reality sets in, and the material looks less brilliant in black and white. Unfortunately, postponing the report causes delays which actually lessen your chances of doing a really bang-up job. In the end, you wind up hating yourself because you waited so long and blew your chances of doing a super paper.

How do you break the procrastinating habit? Here are a few helpful starters:

1. *Force yourself to at least look at the material.* Even if you don't plan to tackle the assignment right away, just glancing at it makes it more familiar to you. The longer you wait to confront a job, the tougher it will seem to get in your mind.

2. *Divide the assignment into small jobs.* Thirty pages of reading and summarizing is a big job in one bite. However, if you do just eight or 10 pages a night, the assignment for the week won't seem so huge.

3. *Work on tasks for short, specific amounts of time.* Just to get going, write down one sentence, no matter how good or bad it is. Or for a reading assignment, read for five minutes — any small thing just to take a quick plunge into the work.

4. *Reward yourself for completing the work.* Promise yourself a good long phone call with a friend after you finish your math problems. Or treat yourself to a television program after you memorize your vocabulary words.

5. *If all else fails, force yourself to choose between doing absolutely nothing or doing the assignment.* Most people can't sit for long without having something to do, and the prospect of working on grammar exercises may seem more appealing than staring at four walls.

A TIME FOR EVERYTHING: HOW TO DETERMINE THE BEST TIME TO DO HOMEWORK

When you set up your homework schedule, think about when you work best. Scientists have learned that people actually have biological clocks their bodies follow. The "owls," as scientists call night people, are the ones who have to drag themselves out of bed in the morning but who work well after the sun goes down. Day people, the "larks," are raring to go in the morning but slow down later in the day. If you happen to be a night person and your family doesn't object to late hours, then plan your homework schedule for nighttime. If you're a lark who has to hit the pillow early, then try to do your homework during your free periods or right after school. Here are some other things to keep in mind about your work schedule:

1. *Pace yourself.* Some students study like mad for the first few weeks of school, then fall apart as the semester goes on. Regular daily studying in even doses is more effective than last-minute, anxious cramming.

2. *Try to study pretty much at the same time and in the same place every day.* You should learn to associate certain times and locations with your study mood. However, don't be a slave to your

schedule, either. Your plans should be flexible enough to allow for those times when a special social or leisure activity comes up. It's also possible to squeeze in short homework tasks in small blocks of time once in a while. Keep your schedule open enough to allow for review time while you're waiting for the bus. Or check over your notes while you wait for class to start.

3. *Plan ahead.* If you have a big test coming up on a certain day, then add a little more time to your schedule the night before for extra review.

How much time should you study every day? As long as it takes you to do a thorough job on your schoolwork and still have time for other things in your life. Some students get everything done in an hour and a half of concentrated study, while others spend three hours fiddling around and still don't complete all the work they have. If you keep falling short of reasonable goals you've set for yourself, then add more study time to your schedule in 15-minute segments until you accomplish what you set out to do. Or try studying at different times of day to see when your concentration is best. Then adjust your work schedule accordingly.

TAKE A SEAT: HOW TO SET UP A WORK PLAN FOR DOING ASSIGNMENTS

Let's assume you've conquered whatever procrastination problems you may have had. You have set aside a couple hours for your assignments, you are ensconced in your study corner with books and materials, and you are ready to roll. How do you actually dive into the work?

1. *Look over your assignment pad and see which assignments are the most difficult.* While it's tempting to save the hardest jobs for last, you should do them when your concentration and energy are at their peaks.

2. *Look over each assignment and ask yourself what you are supposed to get out of it.* A quick glance at that day's notes will refresh your memory about the purpose of the homework.

3. *Do the assignment.* Check the different sections in this book which suggest specific ways to tackle certain kinds of assignments — from reading a textbook to memorizing spelling words.

4. *Go over each assignment as you complete it.* Write notes to yourself or put question marks next to any material you don't understand or cannot complete. Get those points cleared up with your teacher in class the next day.

5. *Treat yourself to five-minute breaks between subjects.*

6. *Check your completed work against the directions in your assignment pad to make sure you've done everything.*

7. *Put all your books and materials where you can find them the next morning.* Then go off and enjoy your free time.

Here is an overall homework checklist to follow until the steps become automatic for you:

Homework Checklist

In-Class Checklist:

☐ You have written down the assignment and its deadline.

☐ You know what books, materials, and information you'll need to complete the assignment.

☐ You understand the purpose of the assignment.

☐ You have asked questions about those parts of the assignment you don't understand.

At-Home Checklist:
For textbook reading assignments:

☐ You've read over the headings and subheadings to see how the material is organized.

☐ You have skimmed the material once to

get a general idea of what it's about.

☐ You have read everything over a second time more slowly.

☐ You have taken notes on important points as you have read.

☐ You have dated your notes and written down the page numbers so that you will know where to find this review material for a test.

For written exercises and workbook assignments:

☐ You have read over the directions twice.

☐ You have skimmed the whole exercise to see what it's about.

☐ You have completed the easiest examples first just to warm up.

☐ You have worked as hard as possible on the more difficult examples.

☐ You have written down questions to ask the teacher about any examples you couldn't complete.

☐ You have read over your assignment to make sure everything is finished, easy to read, and has your name and the date on it.

Wind-up:

☐ You have checked all your completed
work against the directions in your
assignment pad to make sure you've
done everything.

☐ You have gathered your assignments,
books, and notebooks together for
school the next day.

BOOKING IT: HOW TO READ TEXTBOOKS SYSTEMATICALLY

Among other things, textbooks help you
develop strong arm muscles. There's something
a little awesome about getting a textbook on the
first day of class. It's hard to believe you are
going to be responsible for a book that looks so
serious and weighs so much.

There are advantages and drawbacks to using
textbooks in a course. The advantages are these:
All your outside reading for a course is presented
in one place; the information in a text is usually
organized in a chronological way; and once you
get used to the style and organization of the
book, you know what to expect in the rest of the
text. The disadvantages of textbooks are that
they don't always offer the variety and flavor a
selection of several books would; and many texts
are produced by teams of writers and editors, so
the stamp of an individual author is sometimes
absent. In any case, you will be using textbooks

from high school through college, so you should learn the special techniques for reading them.

To use textbooks in the most efficient ways possible, let's go back to their advantages. Since a whole course is often covered in a text, studying its table of contents gives you a sense of the entire semester's scope. Furthermore, the chapters are clearly divided into smaller sections marked in heavy type. These headings preview and outline the material for you in small, easy doses. A good textbook has a detailed index in back for checking specific topics. Think of your textbooks as reference tools rather than as mountains of words you have to conquer. Here's how to reduce that mass of material to something manageable:

1. *Familiarize yourself with the various sections of a textbook:*

   a. The *foreword* or *preface* states the authors' purpose and viewpoint.

   b. The *table of contents* in front outlines the main ideas of each chapter.

   c. The *bibliography* (at the back of the book or at the end of each chapter) lists outside readings related to the subject. Use the bibliography to find books or articles for any research papers your teacher assigns.

   d. The *index* in the back of your book is a page guide to all the topics covered in the text.

2. *Read over the entire table of contents carefully when you first receive your textbook for a course.* This gives you an invaluable overview of what the entire book covers and what direction the course will take.

3. Survey each chapter as it is assigned. This means skimming over the chapter title, the headings, and subheadings in heavy type to get a sense of what the chapter covers and how it is organized. Always do this before you begin your close reading of the chapter.

4. Read the questions at the end of each chapter before you read the chapter. These questions alert you to the authors' main ideas.

5. Pay special attention to words in heavy type, italics, as well as topic sentences, summary paragraphs, or concluding sentences.

6. Take note of any visual information — graphs, tables, diagrams, etc. — displayed in the chapters.

7. Learn to outline textbook chapters if you can't underline in your book. This is fairly easy to do since the headings and subheadings in textbook chapters are already presented for you. Here's an example of how you might outline a typical textbook chapter:

Sample Chapter Outline

Textbook Title: *The Rights of Americans*
Chapter Title: "The Right to Protest" (*main chapter heading*)

  I. Democratic Society Protects Many Forms of

Protest (*subheading from text*)
A. Most traditional forms of protest
    1. Parades
    2. Meetings
    3. Canvassing   (*supporting examples*
    4. Picketing   *of main ideas*
    5. Distribution of literature   *in chapter*)
B. Newer forms of protest
    1. Sit-ins
    2. Shop-ins
    3. Love-ins
II. Current Law (*another subheading from text*)
    A. First Amendment
    B. Government provides   (*supporting*
        protection for   *examples*)
        protestors
III. Place of Protest
    A. Right to use public
        streets, parks, and   (*supporting*
        open spaces.   *examples*)
    B. Supreme courts not yet
        decided in interiors
        of schools, courts,
        or town halls

8. Coordinate your class notes and textbook reading. As you read through your text, fill in any gaps in your class notes with information from the reading. Use your class notes as a guide to help you understand the text.

Here's a special form to follow for your first textbook assignments this year. You don't necessarily have to answer the questions in writing; just thinking about the questions in your head will help you structure your textbook reading so that the steps come automatically.

Textbook Title: _____
Chapter Title: _____

1. What does the chapter title mean?
_____
_____

2. What do I already know about this subject?
_____
_____

3. What information has my teacher given me about this chapter?
_____
_____

4. What do the headings and subheadings mean?
_____
_____
_____
_____

5. What questions do I have about the chapter?
_____
_____
_____
_____

DIFFERENT STROKES: HOW TO DEVELOP SPECIAL STUDY TECHNIQUES FOR EACH SUBJECT

How many times have you thought or heard something like this: "I'm great in English and history, but can't do math"? Some people seem to be whizzes in math and science, but can't spell. Others have no trouble writing until it's time to write out a math problem. While the basic study suggestions we've presented so far — tips on organizing, scheduling, note-taking, and listening — can be applied to all academic areas, there are specific approaches you should develop for different subjects. If you read a novel for English the way you would a textbook, you'll probably never read fiction again. Or if you curl up and read a textbook like a novel, you may develop some peculiar problems with the material.

Each subject has its own vocabulary and viewpoint. While historical events are subject to interpretation, and a Shakespearean sonnet can be appreciated in many ways, the square root of a number or the atomic weight of a chemical element each has a fixed value. Certain memory tricks which help you study spelling and vocabulary words have limited use when it comes to memorizing numbers and dates. So be prepared to change gears as you change subjects.

LOOKING BACK: HOW TO MAKE HISTORY COME ALIVE

History, sociology, anthropology, government, and psychology are generally grouped under the headings "social studies" or "social sciences." Yet the furthest thing from the mind of a history student struggling to memorize dates, battles, names, and places is the thought that people in history ever socialized with one another. Sometimes the study of history reduces interesting historical people to stick figures or turns fascinating events into dates on a calendar (or multiple choice questions on an exam).

History can be a tough subject if names and dates are the focus of the course. On the other hand, a teacher who is excited about history is able to bring characters and events to life. When this happens, students get a full sense of history and still learn where all names and dates fit in. How can you get the most from your history courses in an interesting way?

1. Get the "big picture" at the beginning of the course. One way to preview the entire scope of your course is to study the table of contents, headings, and subheadings in the assigned books. Maintaining this overview gives you a context in which to place the events, dates, and names you will be studying. To keep that chronological picture in your head, reread the table of contents periodically, particularly before exams.

2. Pay close attention to tables, charts, and maps in your book which illustrate the development of ideas and trends. These visual references reinforce your memory of the material in a special way.

3. Learn to associate groups of names, places, and dates. Paul Revere, the Boston Tea Party, and the Battle of Lexington should all ring a bell that says American Revolution. It's a good idea to list clusters of key names and events together, then study from that list for exams.

4. Read novels that fictionalize events of a time period you are studying. You can kill two birds with a single stone by doing book reports for English class on books that cover the same time periods as those you are studying in your history classes. Ask both your teachers for recommendations of related fictional titles.

5. If your history teacher assigns a free-choice research project, try to zero in on something that will bring to life some aspect of the time period you are studying in class. For example, a paper on the design and architecture of the houses, villages, towns, and cities might make a particular period more real to you. Research on the social attitudes toward children and teenagers is an aspect of social history that might offer unusual insights. If you are interested in music, art, crafts, or literature, then investigate what was going on in those areas during a certain time. Check the bibliographies of your textbook for suggestions on social or cultural history topics. The important thing is to personalize history in some way that will make it easier for you to fit in information about a particular time.

6. *Good teachers are interested in exploring the whys and wherefores of history, so try to read your history book with an open, yet critical, mind.* Why did the author of your book choose to present the facts in a particular light? What led up to certain historical events? What connections can you make between historical trends and ideas? Forming your own questions will help you understand how events and people in history affected one another.

7. *A good study tool for both essay and objective history tests is a time line.* Instead of attempting to memorize random dates, get yourself a good long sheet of paper and list the important dates in a line moving down the page. Alongside these dates, write down significant names and key events in your own words. Study from the time line so that the span of history on which you are being tested is in front of you as you review.

8. *Right before a history test, the final things you should check are: your textbook headings, the table of contents covering the test material, and your time line, or any chronological outline you've developed in class or from your textbook.* Each of these things gives you an overview of the material into which you can fit the dates and other details called for on your test.

PICK A NUMBER: HOW TO DEVELOP YOUR MATH SKILLS

The language of mathematics is much more

precise than the written and spoken language you use every day. Students who have a way with words and bluff their way through language arts and social studies often find themselves in hot water when they try the same thing in math. Because mathematics is such an exacting language, there is less leeway for carelessness than in other courses. Missing an important step in math is always critical. For example, it is much harder to figure out a mathematical concept from scratch than it is to learn how to spell a new word on your own. Each step in math builds from the previous one and into the next. Here are some specific approaches you should take toward your math courses:

1. *Learn the vocabulary and rules of mathematics from memory.* Math consists of words as well as numbers, and you can't use its language without knowing the principles and the jargon. Learn exactly what words like *area, volume, perimeter, tangent, progression, rate,* or *factoring* mean. Here is how to memorize mathematical rules and terms:

   a. Read the rule or term silently to yourself. Make sure you understand all the words used in the definitions or rules.
   b. Write a sample of the problem or draw a picture that illustrates the math term. You can do this on index cards or in a special "math dictionary" section of your notebook for quick reference.
   c. Read the definition or rule out loud at least five times until you can "hear" the words in your head. If you have a tape recorder,

read the definitions into a tape, and then see if you can match up the correct terms or rules which apply.

d. Write out math definitions or rules on cards or in the "math dictionary" section of your notebook alongside the illustrations or examples of the term or principle.

2. *If you miss a class, see your teacher at once to make up the work.* Get another student's notes as a back-up.

3. *Get friendly with a classmate who is good in math.* Take advantage of family members who are good in math. Use your math allies to explain things to you.

4. *If your math book is stumping you, see if you can find another one to use as an easy reference.*

5. *Try to connect each new math problem with one you already know.*

6. *Think along with your teacher as she works out problems.* Don't copy any problem down until after your teacher has worked it out and explained it.

7. *Survey each assigned problem.* Determine what it is asking.

8. *Do your homework under test conditions. Time yourself to see how quickly and accurately you can complete each problem under pressure.*

9. *Triple-check each part of your work as you go along.*

10. *Overlearn math concepts.* Even if your teacher is repeating something you already know, stay involved so that you know the concept inside out.

SPEAKING OF SCIENCE: HOW TO STUDY SCIENCE

Generations of biology students have stood over the bodies of generations of frogs and guinea pigs and wondered why these creatures had to lay down their lives for the sake of science. Isn't it possible to get through life without knowing what the inside of an animal looks like? Is it really necessary to know how cells divide, why we breathe, or what photosynthesis is?

From a strictly academic point of view, the study of science strengthens observation skills, stimulates critical thinking, shows you how to conduct experiments and handle scientific equipment. But students who don't get past these basic academic considerations short-change themselves. As with all courses, the more you can relate the material to your own experience, the more you will get from studying it.

In some ways, science resembles math. It has a specialized vocabulary, and it involves problem solving. The scientist or mathematician gets a set of facts, organizes them in an orderly way, develops theories, and tries to work out a solution based on the theories. The guidelines for studying science are similar to those we've already mentioned for studying mathematics. And the methods for reading various textbooks also work for reading a science textbook. Here is how to tackle science in a systematic way:

1. Learn the vocabulary of science. Master scientific terms by memorizing them. One easy way to keep track of these terms is to list them in a "science dictionary" in your notebook or on special cards. This handy reference system is a good study tool at exam time.

2. *Read your science textbook in a systematic way.* Get an overview of your book and the course by studying the table of contents, headings, and subheadings. Determine the main idea and purpose of each chapter by studying the headings and opening and closing paragraphs.

3. *Use what you already know as a basis for learning new material.*

4. *Try to relate every new idea to something in your own experience.* For example, if you are reading about body parts in a physiology course, don't rely only on the illustrations in your book —use your own body as a model for identifying the scientific terms.

5. *Keep in mind that the majority of questions you'll be asked on science exams are these:*

  a. What is the definition of a particular scientific term?

  b. How does a certain structure work?

  c. What is the structure part of?

  d. Draw the structure or label a drawing of the structure.

6. *Follow your teacher's laboratory demonstrations carefully.* These demonstrations show you an idea in action. To get the most from them, here is what to keep in mind:

  a. Listen and note the purpose of the demonstration. What new theory or principle is being shown?

b. How does the demonstration illustrate something you already know?

c. Take down notes on what you see and what the teacher emphasizes.

d. Write down the procedures used as well as the conclusions or generalizations you can make.

7. *Do your own laboratory experiments carefully.* Here's how:

a. Know ahead of time what you are supposed to find out. This information is available in your textbook, lab manual, or your class notes.

b. Follow the directions word for word. If there's something you don't understand, ask the lab instructor about it.

c. Work in a neat, orderly, and systematic way. Make sure you have everything before you begin. Put things down in the same place each time. Don't rush.

d. Keep accurate notes as you perform each step. Don't rely on memory.

e. Write up your experiment completely on the same day you perform it.

SPEAK UP: HOW TO LEARN A FOREIGN LANGUAGE

Two good ways to learn a second language are to grow up in a family that speaks two languages, or win a trip to the foreign country of your choice for several months. The more common alternative is to sign up for a language course in your school. The sooner you are exposed to a new language, the easier it is to study. So don't wait until college to get started.

Schools use a number of techniques for teaching students a second language. Some teachers focus on grammar and introduce the conversational and literary areas later on. Others confound their students on the first day of class by speaking the new language right away. This second method is used to train Peace Corps volunteers and Foreign Service workers. At first, many students are scared off by this total immersion method, and the drop-out rate for those first few days is high. However, studies have shown that the best way to master a language is to live and breathe it for as many hours as possible each day. If you're lucky, you will get a teacher who begins your class with: "Bonjour, ouvrez vos livres, s'il vous plait," or "Por favor habren sus libros," rather than, "Hello, please open your books."

Learning a new language proceeds in specific steps which must each be mastered before moving to the next. You need to know word meanings before you can compose sentences. You have to know about word order and verb tenses before you can translate sentences. Daily systematic preparation and review of your foreign language is absolutely vital. Here are a number of suggestions for mastering the foreign language you are studying:

1. *Read each assignment at least three times.* Skim it at first just to get a general sense of what it

is about. Reread it a second time, going through and noting new words or unfamiliar constructions. During this second reading, look up things you don't understand. Once you have deciphered new words and structures, read the assignment through slowly and carefully a third time.

2. *Learn the new vocabulary.* Follow these steps to develop your vocabulary:

a. Read each new word silently five times.

b. Look away from the new word and say it aloud five times.

c. Read but do not say the English equivalent of the new word.

d. Write the new word down five times on a scrap of paper. Then write it once on a card or in a special "dictionary" section of your notebook.

e. After you have gone through these steps, go back to your list or cards and write a sentence for each of the words. If you can't remember the meaning enough to write a sentence, run through steps a through d again.

If you have a tape recorder, follow all these steps on tape and keep playing back the tape to yourself until you know the new words backwards and forwards. Do not ever write or say meanings of foreign words in English while you are doing your assignments. The point is to get practice in using the original foreign language vocabulary as much as possible. Use your notebook dictionary, cards, or tapes for exam review.

3. *Study the grammar of the new language thor-*

oughly. Understand each rule. Memorize its exact meaning. Use the new rule in speech, assignments, and written work.

4. *Practice and review the new language as often as possible.* Chances are everyone in your class is beginning the language too, so don't be afraid to speak up in class. Regular dialogue and conversation is more fun and more useful than constant rote drills in a new language. Study out loud. Take your language labs seriously. And use a tape recorder, if you have one, to check on your work.

5. *Have some fun with your new language.* Get a pen pal in the country you are studying. Read a magazine or newspaper in your new language once in a while. See films in that language. Read the foreign version of an easy book which you've enjoyed in English. Take out from your library spoken or musical recordings in that language. Even if you don't understand everything you read or listen to, you will start to develop an "ear" for the rhythms of the language.

6. *Start saving money for a trip to the country you are studying.* After all, you should reward yourself for having done all this work!

Chapter 4

PUT TO THE TEST:
How to Take All Kinds of Quizzes and Tests

On the night before any big exam, a predictable number of unprepared students are indulging in a few fantasies. A big blizzard (or hurricane, flood, typhoon, or locust plague) will close down school the next day. Or a strange chemical will be found in the school's chalk dust, and health inspectors will declare the school off-limits. Or perhaps the school secretary will lose the ditto master for the exam and need another day to type up a new one. A large number of students engaging in this type of wishful thinking will fail the test or just squeak by.

On this same pre-exam evening, another group of unprepared students have exhausted all the disaster fantasies and decided to make an

11th-hour effort to cram a semester's work into one night. For the first time in weeks, these students are opening dusty textbooks and preparing themselves for a classic "all nighter." Panic time is on as they race frantically through pages of material assigned ages ago. A large number of C's will go to these students, although a lucky few who thrive on adrenaline will do better.

A small group of test-takers — the planners and studiers — are also reading the material, but not for the first time. These students are reviewing and rechecking notes, textbooks, and other study materials. They are formulating possible test questions in their minds, reciting already-learned information, and feeling fairly confident about the test. Some of these students even have time to read a magazine or watch a little television. These students will write the best exams and earn the highest grades of any group.

Do any of these pre-exam scenarios sound familiar? Most test-takers find themselves in one or another of these groups at some time. The best students stay put in the third group, and that's where you should be before a test.

Tests are given for different reasons. Some teachers use them to determine how well students are learning new material. Others schedule regular tests to get students to review the class work periodically. You should use tests to measure your own strengths and weaknesses in a subject. Tests are unavoidable parts of school life, yet many students never really master the skill of taking them. If what you know about tests is strictly hit or miss, the steps listed below will help you develop a sense of confidence about test-taking.

COUNTDOWN: A STEP-BY-STEP PLAN FOR TEST PREPARATION

Crammers, take note. Imagine what kind of season your baseball, football, or basketball teams would have if all the players waited until the day before each game to start practicing. Steady preparation is the only way to really master any skill, including test-taking. Short sprints are fine as part of your strategy, but shouldn't make up the whole program. Here's how to get yourself in shape for a big test:

1. *Ask your teacher what material will be covered on the test.* Don't waste time reviewing chapters or sections you won't be tested on.

2. *Find out what kind of test will be given — objective, essay, multiple choice, true-false, etc.* As you will see later in this chapter, study techniques vary for each type of test.

3. *In the days or weeks before the exam, listen for clues your teacher gives you about the material.* Underline sections in your notes or reading which tie in with ideas your teacher keeps stressing.

4. *Set up a study schedule to prepare for a big test.* Here's how:

   a. Early in your schedule, catch up on any

reading assignments you may have missed. Skim over all your notes to see if everything is readable and complete. If there are confusing sections, ask your teacher to go over those points. Borrow and copy any notes you don't have. Coordinate your class notes with reading material. Read over previous tests you've taken in the same course. See if you can find other students who have taken the course before and ask them what the tests were like.

b. About a week before the exam, make up any study aids that will help you review the material. These aids should include lists of main ideas, definition sheets or cards, time lines, or concise outlines of the material.

c. Save the last two nights before the test for a final sprint. This is your concentration time. Read all your underlinings and study aids carefully. Reread any materials which have been stressed recently. Do all your memory work in these last two nights.

d. On the night before the exam, make up a list of questions you think will be asked and try to answer them in your head. When you make up these questions, try to think the way your teacher thinks.

5. *Get a good night's sleep.* On test day, look over your study aids calmly. Get to class a little early with all the equipment you need for the test.

These steps outline the preparations you should make for a major exam. For simpler tests, adapt your schedule and condense the steps into a night or two of study. If you've been doing your assignments all along, the final preparations for any test should go smoothly and quickly.

One last word. Don't skip tests, or if you have to miss one, make it up as soon as possible. Although teachers usually hate giving make-ups, it's better to take one than settle for a zero. Take a look at how a zero from a missed test affects the rest of your grade. Let's assume your grades for tests and papers have been 90, 85, 75, and 80, and you get a 70 on your last test. Your average for the semester will be 80. If you miss the last test and average a zero into 90, 85, 75, and 80, your grade goes down to 66.

TRICKS OF THE TRADE: SPECIAL TEST PREPARATION TECHNIQUES

By the time you graduate from high school, you will have learned some nifty shortcuts for taking notes, writing papers, and passing tests. If you go to college, at the end of four years you will have picked up even more inside tricks on how to get through school without taking a lot of detours. Finally, by the time you've finished school, you'll have a whole repertoire of school survival techniques. While you're still in the process of coping with school demands, here are some shortcuts for test-taking to use right now:

1. *How to improve your memory* — Memories

are made of bits and pieces of information you have to pull from your brain under pressure. The steps involved in sharpening your memory for schoolwork aren't much more complicated than those you would follow to memorize a phone number. You hear it, you write it down, or you keep repeating the digits until you can dial the sequence automatically. The process for memorizing rules, spelling words, math problems, or definitions takes longer but involves the same steps.

Here are a few tips to help you improve your memory:

a. Understand what you are trying to memorize. If a textbook term stumps you, for example, check an easy-to-read dictionary for a simpler definition. If you can't figure out what a passage, process, or rule is all about, find out what it means from your teacher before you attempt to memorize it.

b. Write down what you are trying to memorize. This is the phone-number trick again. Of course, if what you are trying to remember is long and involved, then skip the writing step and go to Step c.

c. Repeat out loud what you are attempting to memorize. Why are TV commercial jingles or song lyrics so easy to remember? Because you keep hearing them over and over. Keep repeating the material you want to learn until you can practically say it backwards and forwards. Again, a tape recorder is a big help in memory work. Record what you're trying to learn into a tape, then keep playing it back.

Just for fun, leave blank spots in parts of the tape and see if you can fill them in on your own. If family members or friends are available, have them read off key words from your material to see if they trigger off what you need to know. Keep working aloud until the information comes as easily as one of those jingles.

d. Break down passages and paragraphs into sentences or single words as you memorize.

e. Do your memory exercises in small blocks of time. Figure out your attention span, then only work for that amount of time on memorization.

f. Read and reread what you are trying to memorize. Do this until you start to get a "picture" of the words or passages in your head.

g. Associate what you are trying to learn with something you already know. How is that new vocabulary word like one you've already memorized? How is that tricky spelling word similar to words you know how to spell?

2. *How to organize a study group* — Sometimes before a test, two or more heads are better than one, providing that the heads in question are really studying and not just shooting the breeze. If you have one or two studious friends in class, collaboration with them can be a great way to prepare for a big exam. Here is how to organize and use a study group advantageously:

a. Get together as soon as your exam date is set. Sit down with your group and plan a schedule and a strategy. Assign each person a special section of the material to work on. This means writing up a short summary of the section, listing its main ideas, and formulating a few likely questions about the material. Of course, all the group members have to study the rest of the material as well, but the concentrated work can be done individually. Each member should produce copies of notes on her area for everyone else in the group. A couple nights before the test, the group should meet again to pool all the information, predict questions, and answer them aloud in detail.

3. *How to pre-test yourself* — Anticipating what a test will cover is the best way to get in gear for exam day. If you've taken other tests in the course, you should reread them before you study for the current test. Think about the kinds of questions your teacher asks in class, then form similar questions about the material under study. If you are getting an essay test, try to come up with a few likely questions, then do a short outline that addresses itself to each one. Work out a few key math or science problems on paper as a pre-test warm-up. Test yourself out loud in spelling, vocabulary, or grammar. Do all your pre-testing exercises as close to the test date as possible.

4. *Cramming* — Cramming may be hazardous to your health. Think of what would happen to your digestive system if you ate a week's worth of food in one meal. Sounds pretty disgusting, doesn't it? Yet cramming — that old school standby—is the mental version of that stuffing process. While it's self-destructive to count on cramming to get you through a course, it beats

not studying at all. Keeping in mind that cramming should only be used as a last resort, here is how to use an 11th-hour sprint in the most efficient way possible:

a. Concentrate. The pressure of a big exam bearing down is the only way some people can really get down to business before a test. A panicky countdown makes many procrastinators shape up fast.

b. Read your notes first to get a sense of what your teacher emphasized in class. This gives you an approach to the rest of the material if you have time to get to it. Reread three times anything you underlined or starred in these notes.

c. Go to your class text. Carefully read all the titles and subtitles at least three times. If you have time, quickly skim the material. If there's no time, just read the headings, opening and closing paragraphs of each section, and any points which were emphasized in class.

d. If you're being tested on rules, definitions, or spelling, read each term or word silently five times, then aloud five times.

e. If you're going to be tested on math or science problems, pick out two or three typical examples which have been stressed in class and work them out as quickly as possible on paper.

f. If you're being tested on novels and stories you've never read at all, you are in deep trouble. The only thing you can do is reread your class notes on that material, then try to get some sense of the book by reading the first and last chapters or sections, as well as one chapter or section which has been stressed in class.

g. Get some sleep. Even a little sleep will help you process information better. Researchers have found that concentrated study followed by a few hours of sleep works far better than a sleepless marathon session right up to the exam. Without any sleep, you'll be a zombie, and your chances of totally blanking out will be astronomical.

h. Obviously, these jamming techniques are slap-dash attempts at best. If you cram, you are going to wind up with lots of blank spots in your knowledge. When you do get to the test, spend the most time developing what you do know instead of trying to fake your way through things you know nothing about. A few solid answers may balance out those questions you can't answer at all. Finally, if you are going to cram, pay special attention to the next section on how to tackle different kinds of tests.

OFF AND RUNNING: TAKING THE TEST

Whether you've been a steady test reviewer or a last-minute crammer, the moment of truth arrives when your teacher hands out that blue-inked piece of paper. For some students, that moment triggers off paralysis. For others, it sets a kind of creative adrenaline flowing, and they're off and running. The steps below outline the way you should address yourself to the test at hand:

1. *First, be on time and well equipped.* Once the class begins, put away all your notes and try to focus your thoughts. Take a few, slow, deep breaths. Close your eyes for a moment. If you draw a blank when you get the test, do more deep breathing. Turn the test sheet over and doodle leisurely for a moment or two just to get your pen moving as you gather your thoughts. Turn the paper back to the front and write down your name, the class, and the date.

2. *From the moment you get the test, listen carefully to your teacher's comments.* Have him repeat directions if necessary. Ask questions. If something seems unclear after you have begun, bring your paper up to the teacher and ask him to explain the confusing section to you.

3. *Skim the directions once to get a sense of what is required.* Read them a second time and underline any important words. Then read the instructions slowly a third time in order to fix them in your mind for the duration of the test. Here are some things to look for in a set of test directions:

    a. Time allotment—How much time do you have for the whole test?

    b. Choices — Must you answer all or only some of the questions? Can you choose from a selection of topics on an essay test?

    c. Scoring — Are certain questions worth more than others? If so, plan your schedule and test strategy accordingly.

    d. Form of the questions — Do you check, fill-in, underline, cross out, match, or circle answers? Do you answer true-false, yes or no, or do you complete statements?

e. Materials — Can you use scrap paper, notes, a dictionary, calculator, etc.?

4. *Quickly figure out a schedule for the test.* Write out your mini-schedule in the top corner of the sheet, or mark the time allotment you plan to set aside for each question. If certain questions are worth more than others, set aside proportionately more time for those.

5. *Skim all the test questions to get a sense of what your teacher is asking.* Tackle the easiest questions first in order to score as many points as possible early on.

6. *Read each question three times and underline the key words in each.* Here's a list of them:

all	always	never	better
every	often	more	best
most	usually	equal	bad
many	sometimes	less	worse
few	seldom	fewer	worst
none	rarely	good	

7. *Guess answers if you won't be penalized for doing so.*

8. *Go back and answer any questions you skipped during your first run-through.*

9. *Double-check your answers.* Don't change any unless you have a very good reason for doing so.

10. *Learn from your mistakes.* When you get back your corrected exam, read it over carefully and see what your strong and weak points are. If you don't understand where you went wrong on certain items, ask your teacher to explain those

examples. Save all your corrected tests in a folder. When the next test comes up, use your old tests as a study tool to plan your next strategy.

TESTING, TESTING, ONE, TWO, THREE: HOW TO TAKE DIFFERENT KINDS OF TESTS

There are nearly as many different kinds of tests as there are teachers to administer them. Some teachers prefer the objective test—the kind which requires a definite right answer and can be scored quickly. Teachers who want to stir up your creative juices give subjective tests which ask you to express opinions about the assigned material in a more personal way. While these are harder to take and more difficult for a teacher to correct, subjective tests are a lot more challenging than true-false, fill-in, and matching tests. Mid-term and final exams are often a mix of the two types. As you prepare for tests, adapt your study techniques to the type of test your teacher is planning to give.

Your objective on an objective test is to supply, recall, or recognize as many right answers as possible. Facts, details, names, dates, terms, and definitions should be the focus of your test preparation. Objective tests include the following:

1. *The true-false test* asks you to verify whether a statement is right or wrong or to select one of

two statements as true or false.

a. Test preparation: Go over facts, definitions, dates, rules, and important statements stressed in your text and in class. Memory work is important here.

b. Test procedures: Read the directions three times, underlining important words. Scan all the questions to get a sense of the whole test. Tackle the easy items first. Read the first statement quickly but carefully. Write in your answer immediately if it comes to you right away. Go through all the easy examples in this way. Put a question mark next to those you skip. On a second run-through, guess at questions you missed before if your teacher is only counting right answers (this is the usual case). Put a double question mark next to those you still can't figure out. Again, if you won't be penalized for wrong answers, take a wild guess at the double-marked examples if you have time. Don't change answers during your final review unless you have a very good reason.

c. Test tips: Be alert to these word clues in true-false questions: "all," "none," "only," "generally," "always," "never," "more likely," "unlikely," "probably," "seldom." Don't dwell on any single question as you move through this type of test since time is an important element. Keep in mind that if any part of a statement is false, the entire statement is false. Often there are more true statements than false since it's easier for a teacher to pull out exact statements from the assigned material than make up false ones.

2. *The multiple-choice* test is a true-false test
with more choices. Here you have to choose the
truest statement from the options. Because there
are more choices, this type of test is trickier than a
straight true-false type.

a. Test preparation : Study facts, dates, important statements, and definitions which
have been stressed in class and assigned material. As you review, try to connect words,
facts, phrases, and ideas together. Pre-test
yourself by saying or writing a key word.
Then think of as many associated words and
phrases as you can.

b. Test procedure: Read the directions three
times, making sure to underline important
words as you read them. Scan all of the questions on the test to get a sense of your teacher's
purpose. Go to the easiest questions first and
read them carefully. Underline the clue words
(see page 95). In your head, try to reason out
the correct answer before you read the
choices. Then see if you can locate an answer
similar to the one you thought of. If not, then
eliminate the obviously false choices. After
you run through the easy questions, work on
the more difficult ones. Simplify the questions
by putting them in your own words. See if you
can break down the hard examples into small
parts.

c. Test tips: Check for grammatical consis-
tency in the choices. Do the verb tenses match
up with the original? Do the choices agree in
number with the first part of the statement?

Clue words on multiple-choice tests include: "best," "most," "least," "correct," "incorrect," "right," "wrong."

3. *The matching test* asks you to associate related ideas, terms, and statements.

a. Test preparation: Focus on connecting words, facts, and phrases in your review. Pretest yourself for a matching test by listing a column of important terms. Then write in as many related words and phrases as possible in the next column.

b. Test procedure: Read the directions three times, underlining important words as you go along. Scan both columns quickly. Then work down one column at a time. Choose the column with the longest phrases because it will contain more clues. Do the easiest items first to narrow down the examples. As you answer questions, cross them out (unless items can be used more than once). After completing the items you know, go back and take a guess at matching the remaining examples. Check over your work to see if you've completed everything. Avoid changing answers without good reason.

c. Test tips: Names of people are generally associated with their notable achievements or actions. Laws or rules are generally associated with their dates of origin, founders, or function. Locations are usually related to important events that happened there.

4. *The fill-in test* asks you to complete a statement with a logical word or phrase.

a. Test preparation: Spend time reviewing

and memorizing facts. Read or list important factual statements but block out the ending and see if you can fill it in with an appropriate word or phrase.

b. Test procedure: Read over the directions three times, underlining important words as you go along. Scan the entire test, then go back to the easiest questions and read each one carefully. In the margin, list as many associated words as you can think of which could complete the statement. Then try out each one with the main part of the question. Write in the answer that looks most familiar in the blank. Run through the test again and try to answer the harder questions by reasoning them through.

c. Test tips: Use grammatical clues. For example, if "an" precedes the blank, the answer begins with a vowel sound. Coordinate number and tenses of possible answers with the main part of the example.

The short and long essay exams are considered subjective tests. This means they are subject to your teacher's interpretation. Right and wrong answers are not as important as well-written statements on major ideas. Since your teacher's interpretation is a big factor on an essay exam, try to determine her special theories, biases, and pet peeves about the material. Here's a rundown on the preparation and procedures you should follow for a long essay exam:

5. *An essay exam* requires your in-depth exploration of major themes. You are expected to sup-

port your statements with material from the course work and make connections between ideas.

a. Test preparation: Forget about cramming if you want to do well on an essay test. It demands a clear grasp of the highlights of the course. To get this overview, study the underlined sections of your notes and read your textbook with a special emphasis on titles, headings, and subheadings. On a final run-through of the reading, make a list of the main ideas you find, along with supporting facts and examples from the material. Right before the exam, make up a list of possible essay questions and see how well you can formulate answers for each of them. Patch up any holes in your knowledge during this step.

b. Test procedure: Read the directions three times, underlining key words as you go over them. Scan the entire test and select the easiest examples. Budget time for each question. Read each question carefully and underline the clue words before you start writing. On a piece of scrap paper or on the other side of the sheet, write down every detail, example, or fact you associate with the question. Then organize this information into a short outline or chronological list. With your outline before you, write a clear introductory sentence stating your main idea. The rest of your essay should develop and support this topic through facts, examples, and related ideas. Make sure each paragraph makes only one point.

c. Test tips: Develop and expand what you know and don't spend time writing about what you don't know. Sprinkle your essay with key phrases, terms, and statements from the teacher's lectures. Focus on opening and closing paragraphs since these will make the most lasting impressions. Be alert to these clue words on an essay exam:

compare	interpret
contrast	justify
criticize	list
define	outline
describe	prove
diagram	relate
discuss	review
evaluate	state
explain	summarize
illustrate	

6. *The short-essay test* asks you to cover a single topic in one paragraph.

a. Test prepartion: Draw up a list of possible test topics as you review class notes and reading. Formulate questions about each subject and see how much information you can recall to answer them. Memorize facts and examples to use as supporting material.

b. Test procedure: Read the directions carefully, particularly noting the number of questions you have to answer. Scan the test and check off the easiest examples. Budget time for each question. Underline key words as you read each one. (See the list of essay clue words above.) On a scrap of paper or on the reverse side of the test sheet, make a short list of all the specific details you can relate to the question. Number these items in order of importance. (There's usually no time to do a real outline on a short-essay test.) Develop a good topic sentence about the number-one point you noted. Use the rest of the items in two or three supporting sentences.

c. Test tips: Your topic sentence must hit the nail on the head. Spend time on it. Make sure you include at least one important accurate fact in your supporting sentences.

When your teacher returns the corrected exam, go over it carefully. Use it to develop your strategy for future tests. Put it in your test folder, then relax and forget about tests for a while.

Chapter 5

THE PAPER CHASE: Writing All Kinds Of Papers

BLOCK AND TACKLE: HOW TO GET STARTED WRITING

If you've ever stared at a blank piece of paper and hoped for brilliant words to appear by magic, you know what it means to suffer from writer's block. It's a common ailment, and the only cure for it is writing. Putting something down is the most effective way of coping with that blank sheet of paper.

Sometimes writer's block is really a topic problem. The writer doesn't know what to write about or how to deal with an assigned subject.

Although teachers generally suggest specific topics, this can be a mixed blessing. While it guarantees the subject is something the teacher actually wants, sometimes an assignment topic limits student writers. The topic may be unfamiliar or uninteresting, or it may be too broad or lacking in potential.

Before you begin work on an assigned topic, develop an angle for it; find a way of putting your personal stamp on it. Imagine two reporters investigating a fire. One reporter writes about the devastated building, the number of people routed from their beds, the extent of the damage, and the number of fire fighters at the scene. Another reporter, covering the same fire, focuses instead on the effect of the disaster on a single family. This reporter describes how one child left behind her teddy bear; how the family lost everything it had; how the tragedy was yet another serious setback in their lives. Getting an angle means developing a personal viewpoint about the material.

If your teacher assigned a paper on the labor laws at the turn of the century, you could investigate the abuses which existed at that time. Or you could track down books describing what family life was like when even young children had to work. You might even recreate what a typical work day was like for a 10-year-old child.

Juvenile delinquency is a topic social-studies teachers often assign. What can you do with a topic that broad? Narrow it down. What happens to young offenders in your community? What are local correctional facilities like? How do these teenagers spend their days? Looking at this broad topic in special ways would involve footwork, interviews, and research, but would also personalize the topic for you.

What do you do when you're stuck on a topic or have to come up with one of your own?

1. *Look at the topic straight on, inside out, upside down.* List all it possibilities and choose an angle that has the most potential.

2. *Talk to your teacher about the topic.* See if she can suggest some interesting aspects.

3. *See your school librarian for suggestions.* Check whether your library has any interesting books on the subject. If your topic is a current one, check *The Readers' Guide* for articles that might suggest new approaches.

4. *Brainstorm with classmates.* Here are the rules for brainstorming:

   a. Each person comes to a group session with a few possible ideas about the topic.

   b. Members offer one idea at a time to the group. Everyone writes down each idea as it comes up. During this time, no one is allowed to criticize or comment on the ideas no matter how impossible or unworkable they seem. The idea of brainstorming is to get everyone contributing without fear of criticism. Ideally, brainstorming sets off a whole string of good ideas right during the session. The exchange continues until all ideas are exhausted.

   c. At the end, the group discusses each idea on the list. This is the time to talk about the possibilities and limitations of the suggested topics.

d. The members choose from among the ideas for their papers.

The bigger the brainstorming group, the better, but even two people can brainstorm together. Your teacher may be willing to conduct a session in class; if not, just get together with one or two classmates and organize a session on your own.

5. Use oddball reference books in the library to get ideas. *The Book of Lists; The Dictionary of Misinformation; The Encyclopedia of Ignorance; The People's Almanac; The Guinness Book of World Records; Ripley's Believe It or Not; How Things Work; The Best, the Worst, and the Most Unusual* are full of off-the-wall ideas that will get you out of the topic rut. In recent years, new encyclopedias on jokes, comics, music, television, and movies have been published. Ask your librarian to recommend offbeat or purely entertaining reference books.

To prove that even the most boring topic has its creative possibilities, here's what a student could do with a subject universally regarded as the dullest writing topic of all time, "My Summer Vacation":

"During my summer vacation, war broke out between two countries." (Proceed with a paper on foreign affairs.)

"Over my summer vacation, I spent nearly 800 hours sound asleep in beds, hammocks, chairs, and tents." (Follow through with a piece on the art of taking a nap.)

"During my summer vacation, I decided all school buildings should be air-conditioned."

(Proceed with a first-person narrative on going to summer school.)

"Over my summer vacation, approximately 1,700 ice-cream cones found their way out of Hinkle's Ice Cream Parlour." (Follow through with an offbeat article on the eating habits of ice-cream lovers.)

APPLAUSE, APPLAUSE: HOW TO FIND YOUR AUDIENCE

Writing without an audience is like putting on a play in an empty theater. The point of writing is to communicate, and that can only happen when two or more people share information.

Most writing books stress the importance of writing for a particular audience. While this is good advice for a widely-read writer, a student writer has to settle for an audience of one — the teacher. Your first step is to make that an audience of two — you and your teacher. Never write a paper you wouldn't enjoy reading yourself. Chances are you like reading interesting and well-written work. If you try to meet those standards in your own writing, you'll wind up satisfying your other audience as well — the teacher who will be reading your work.

FOLLOW THE LEADER: HOW TO WRITE A LEAD SENTENCE

Lead sentences are tough to write. They have to do several jobs: hook the reader, present the topic, set the tone, and control the other sentences in the paragraph. News reporters usually write the most informative leads because they have to present the most vital facts first. Here are a few suggestions for developing this special skill:

1. *Develop an eye for good lead sentences as you read articles, essays, and first lines in published works.* Here are a few examples of well-written leads which Donald Murray cites in his book, *A Writer Teaches Writing*:

"There is something to be said for a bad education." (Phyllis McGinley, *The Province of the Heart*.)

"As I write, highly civilized human beings are flying overhead trying to kill me." (George Orwell, *A Collection of Essays*.)

"The biggest shadow in the world — 235,000 miles high, 105 miles wide, and 75 miles thick in its densest part — fell across San Diego today, the shadow of the moon as it crossed the face of the sun." (Magner While, in a Pulitzer Prize-winning story, *San Diego Sun*, September 10, 1923.)

"Snow, followed by small boys on sleds." (H. Allen Smith, *New York World Telegram* weather forecast.)

2. *Zero in on your topic in your lead sentence or use it as a teaser to make the reader want to read on.*

3. *Write at least three different versions of a lead sentence.*

4. *Choose the lead which seems to offer the most possibilities.*

FOUNDATIONS: HOW TO BUILD A GOOD PARAGRAPH

Lewis Carroll and James Joyce are two of a very small number of authors who managed to get by without using paragraphs in some of their writing. But unless you've got *Through the Looking Glass* or *Finnegan's Wake* under wraps for your teacher, it's important for you to learn how to write a well-constructed paragraph.

A good paragraph advances your topic step by step. The topic sentence presents your main idea, supporting sentences develop it, and the concluding sentence ties up everything in recap of the main idea. Donald Murray has devised several models of well-built paragraphs in his book, *A Writer Teaches Writing*. These are just three examples of how to construct a paragraph.

Topic sentences documented by supporting sentences:

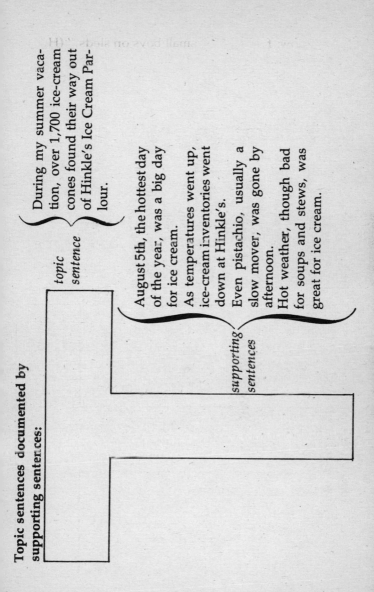

topic sentence

During my summer vacation, over 1,700 ice-cream cones found their way out of Hinkle's Ice Cream Parlour.

supporting sentences

August 5th, the hottest day of the year, was a big day for ice cream.

As temperatures went up, ice-cream inventories went down at Hinkle's.

Even pistachio, usually a slow mover, was gone by afternoon.

Hot weather, though bad for soups and stews, was great for ice cream.

**Supporting sentences
lead to main idea:**

*supporting
sentences*

Hot weather, though bad for soups and stews, was great for ice cream last summer.

As temperatures went up, ice-cream inventories went down at Hinkle's Ice Cream Parlour.

August 5th, the hottest day of the year, was a big day for ice cream.

Even pistachio, usually a slow mover, was gone by afternoon.

*topic
sentence*

Over the summer, more than 1,700 ice-cream cones found their way out of Hinkle's.

108

Supporting sentences lead to main idea then document it:

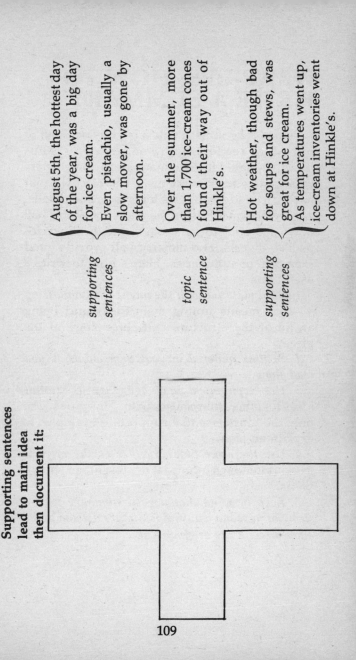

supporting sentences

> August 5th, the hottest day of the year, was a big day for ice cream.
> Even pistachio, usually a slow mover, was gone by afternoon.

topic sentence

> Over the summer, more than 1,700 ice-cream cones found their way out of Hinkle's.

supporting sentences

> Hot weather, though bad for soups and stews, was great for ice cream.
> As temperatures went up, ice-cream inventories went down at Hinkle's.

WRAP-UPS: HOW TO WRITE A SUMMARY

Reader's Digest has made a big business out of providing readers with condensed or summarized material. Summaries are for readers who want a quick overview of a subject without having to wade through a lot of facts and details. A good summary helps the reader or writer boil down material to its basic elements. Encyclopedias, digests, and almanacs all provide good examples of summaries. Here's how to write a useful one:

1. *Read material with the intent of summarizing it.* That means noting main ideas and being aware of the structure and chronology of the piece.

2. *Rethink material in your own words as you read along.*

3. *Use economical language.* Group similar ideas together. Join clauses with semicolons. Use only the most essential supporting examples to explain an idea.

4. *Use the same time structure as the original work.* If it moves from past to present, so should yours.

5. *Keep in mind that a good summary isn't a string of facts but a unified miniature version of the main ideas in the original source.*

CRITICS' CHOICE: HOW TO WRITE A CRITIQUE

Imagine getting paid for your opinions. That's how critics make a living, and some of the more powerful of them make or break movies, books, plays, and records as well.

You will almost never see a published critique that says, "Well, that movie wasn't so hot." Or, "I don't know. I just didn't like it." Good critics try to prove their arguments by giving the reader specific examples from the work which show why something provoked a particular reaction.

From time to time, teachers will ask you to express your judgments in a critical essay. Here is how to organize and write one:

1. *Make a list of all your opinions about the subject.* Next to each opinion write down one example from the material that supports the opinion.

2. *Rearrange your opinions and examples in an outline or numbered list that shows the order you plan to follow.*

3. *With your outline or list before you, work on a lead sentence.* This should really grab your reader's attention and leave no doubt as to where you stand on your subject.

4. *Show, don't tell.* Write supporting sentences and paragraphs which show exactly why you have certain opinions about the material.

5. *Finally, in a concluding sentence, restate your main idea.*

6. *Proofread your critique.* (See the proofreading checklist on page 132.)

BOOKKEEPING: HOW TO WRITE A BOOK REPORT

First, read the book. An amazing number of book reports are based on rehashed class notes, purchased plot summaries, or movie versions of novels. While some teachers may be oblivious to plagiarized material, others are insightful about who read what. And as far as movie versions of books go, keep in mind that local television stations are notorious for cutting out key scenes and lines. More than one student over the years has received back a faked report with comments similar to: "Sorry, this is a movie review, not a book report on *Wuthering Heights*. The 1939 version (which I also watched Saturday night) is nothing like the book. Please read the book and rewrite this report. Signed, Your Teacher."

So, read the book. As you read it, take brief notes on the characters, settings, and plot development. It takes just a few minutes and will save you a lot of time when you go to organize your report. Here are some tips for writing good book reports:

1. *Get in the habit of reading book reviews. Time, Newsweek, Seventeen, Glamour,* and *Mademoiselle* magazines run excellent book reviews in each issue. Professional critics don't usually rely on plot summaries but focus on an angle that gives the reader a flavor of the entire book. This is what you should be working for in your own reports.

2. *Determine the kind of book report your teacher wants, then adjust your reading to the assignment.* Does she expect you to focus on characters? If so, underline passages that reveal the characters' personalities. Does she want you to consider the author's style? Then note important descriptive or narrative passages. Is plot development what your teacher is after? Then develop a plot line as you read.

3. *Write down the main ideas, themes, or scenes that struck you as you read.* Do this as soon as you finish the book. Use this list as the basis of your report.

4. *Try to think of a small but interesting aspect of the book to develop in your report.* Draw from your list of main ideas. Is the writer a humorist? If so, track down comic examples or incidents in the book to use as supporting material for your opinions.

5. *Draw up a plan for your report.* Do a character outline if that's the point of your report. Develop a plot outline if that's where you're headed.

6. *With your outline or plan before you, work on a good opening sentence for the report.* Support your topic sentence with specific examples and quotations from the book.

7. *Write a conclusion that wraps up what you've said.* Leave the reader with a definite idea of whether or not to read the book. Remember, you can totally pan a book provided you do it with insight, style, and proof of what you're saying.

8. *Read over your rough draft carefully — preferably aloud — to see if everything moves smoothly*

from one point to the next.

9. Rewrite your rough draft.

10. Proofread your final copy. (See proofreading checklist on page 132.)

ON THE SCENE: HOW TO WRITE A SHORT REPORT

From time to time your teacher will ask you to focus on a small, interesting aspect of a subject. When your teacher assigns a short report, say three or four pages of writing, the smaller you make your topic the better. Keep narrowing down your subject until you can't make it any smaller. For example, if your teacher asks you to discuss the culture of the 1960's in some way, it would be inadvisable to try to cover the highlights in just a few pages. However, you could focus in on hairstyles or clothing styles of that decade as a way of treating the topic. Think small for the short report. Here are some other tips to keep in mind for this type of assignment:

1. Pick a topic you know something about. That way you won't have to do much research on it. If you are a comic-book collector, you could probably write a short paper on the development of one superhero. If you are a potter, you might want to consider a report on a certain type of Indian water vessel.

2. List everything you can think of or find on your topic.

3. Cross out what you don't plan to use from your

list. Number the remaining items in order of importance.

4. *Make up a short outline or numerical list in the order you plan to follow.*

5. *With the outline or list before you, start working on your lead sentence.* Spend most of your time on this. When you get a good one, you'll know it because the rest of the material will seem to fall into place.

6. *Develop the body of the paper with information and opinions which support your lead sentence.* The body of the report will consist of paragraphs that expand and explain your first paragraph.

7. *Write your conclusion.* This paragraph should summarize and restate your main idea in a new way.

8. *Proofread your paper.* (See the proofreading sheet on page 132.)

WRITE IT RIGHT: HOW TO WRITE AN ESSAY PAPER

The essay paper is really a take-home essay exam, and many of the requirements for writing them are the same. In both, you are expected to develop major themes from your course, support them with specific details, and make connections among important ideas. On an essay paper, however, your teacher will expect more because of the extra time you will have to work on it.

Before moving on to the game plan for writing

an essay paper, take a look at the different types of essays you may be assigned. Let's assume your teacher asks you to write an essay on how rhythm and blues affected the development of rock and roll. Here are some methods for developing that topic:

Methods of Development:

Examples:

1. essay by definition

What is rhythm and blues? What is rock and roll?

2. essay by comparison and contrast

Discuss similarities and differences between rhythm and blues and rock and roll.

3. essay by facts and figures

Where did each type of music originate? Who were the first musicians to develop each type? What was the following for each? Sales figures now?

4. essay by persuasive argument

What is your opinion of each type? Defend your opinion with specifics.

5. essay by proving a point

Why is one kind of music superior to the other?

6. essay by anecdote	Tell about the developments of each type through stories.
7. essay by criticism	Focus on the strengths or weaknesses of each type of music.
8. essay by summary	Trace the chronological development of each type.
9. essay by relationships	How are these two kinds of music similar or dissimilar to other types of music?

If your teacher assigns an essay topic without suggesting a particular approach, choose a method from this list which will work best for you. Once you decide on an angle and a method of development, here's what to do next:

1. *Do some research on your topic if you need more information.* This research may suggest new ideas or other approaches. Again, if you've chosen to write on something familiar, your research for an essay paper won't take long.

2. *Write down everything you associate with your topic.* List your opinions and write supporting examples below them. Cross out those you decide not to use.

3. *Put your list in order.* You can do this on cards, an outline, or a numerical list of ideas.

4. *With your outline or list before you, work on*

your topic sentence. This is the key to an essay paper or test. Spend a lot of time on it.

5. *Develop and write the main body of your essay*. These paragraphs should support your topic sentence.

6. *Write your concluding paragraph*. Remember this is a summary of what you've already said, but it's stated in another way that leaves your reader with a clear impression of what the whole essay is about.

7. *You now have a rough draft*. Go over it. This is your last chance to add things you may have forgotten or cut out things that don't advance your topic effectively. At this point, read your draft aloud to yourself or into a tape recorder. How does it move along? Smooth out sentences. Work on transitions between paragraphs. Check over grammar and spelling.

8. *Rewrite your paper with the new changes*.

9. *Proofread your essay*. (See proofreading checklist on page 132.)

FINAL CUT: THE LAST WORD ON WRITING PAPERS

What all your papers require is a clear statement of your main idea, supporting material that develops this idea, and a conclusion that leaves your reader with a definite impression of what you have said. These principles apply equally to paragraphs, short reports, or lengthy essays.

They are the foundation of all kinds of writing. If you have that logical framework, everything else is simple by comparison.

You find a topic, you gather your thoughts and material on it, you organize a plan of attack, you write, you rewrite, and you polish everything at the end. You double-check that your writing is neat and readable, then you turn it in with the confidence that you gave the topic your best shot.

Chapter 6

CHECK IT OUT: School Survival Checklists And Forms

TOOLS OF THE TRADE: A SCHOOL EQUIPMENT CHECKLIST

The Necessities:

☐ Two or three copies of your class schedule (one for home, another for your notebook, and one for your locker)

☐ A three-ring notebook with dividers for each subject

☐ An assignment pad

☐ A large supply of notebook paper (half at home; the rest in your notebook or locker)

- [ ] A supply of pens and pencils (half at home; the rest in your locker)
- [ ] A good dictionary
- [ ] A thesaurus
- [ ] The phone number of one student in each of your classes (Swap numbers with a classmate so you can exchange notes or other class information after absences.)
- [ ] A library card
- [ ] A wristwatch

Optional:
- [ ] An alarm clock or clock radio
- [ ] A bookbag, knapsack, or tote bag
- [ ] A cassette tape recorder
- [ ] Earplugs
- [ ] Pocket calendar, wall calendar, or bulletin board

ON TIME

	Sun.	Mon.	Tues.	Wed.	Thurs.	Fri.	Sat.
9:00							
10:00							
11:00							
12:00							
1:00							
2:00							
3:00							
4:00							
5:00							
6:00							
7:00							
8:00							
9:00							
10:00							
11:00							

HEAR, HEAR: A LISTENING SKILLS CHECKLIST

☐ Read your work before going to class.
☐ Be on time.
☐ Leave personal problems outside.
☐ Sit close to the front of the room if you can.
☐ Wear glasses or contact lenses to class if you have them.
☐ Be alert to opening and closing remarks. (Main points are usually made during introductions and conclusions.)
☐ Listen for "buzz" words.

Openers:
"First,...Second,...Third,..."
"A major development..."
"Remember that..."
"Take note of..."
"Notice that..."
"The basic idea is..."
"Now this is important..."
"The reason is this..."

Supporting Material:
"For example..."
"For instance..."
"Furthermore..."
"As an example..."
"Similarly..."
"In contrast..."
"On the other hand..."
"Also...,"

Conclusions:
  "Finally..."
  "In summary..."
  "As a result"
  "From this we can see..."
  "Therefore..."
  "In conclusion..."

☐ Follow the teacher's body language (facial expressions, gestures, etc.) and listen for changes in tone of voice. (Gestures and voice are used to emphasize important points.)
☐ Form silent questions about the material.
☐ Reinforce what you hear with good notes.
☐ Borrow someone else's notes to cover any points you didn't hear clearly.

TAKE NOTE: A NOTE-TAKING CHECKLIST

☐ Preview main points in pre-class assignments.
☐ Date each day's notes and write the name of the class.

☐ Leave margins for notes to yourself. Leave space at the bottom of each set of notes to add other material.

☐ Record only main ideas. (Your teacher signals these in opening and closing remarks, buzz words, repetition, board demonstrations, and physical emphasis.)

☐ Arrange main ideas in headings. (An outline is the best form to follow for this.)

☐ Write examples and supporting information under the main ideas.

☐ Call attention to important words with personal symbols. (Question marks, boxes, lines, arrows, stars, etc.)

☐ Use abbreviations or your own shorthand symbols if you understand them. (See page 45.)

☐ Borrow back-up notes from a classmate if you miss a class or happen to take unclear notes during a particular class.

ON ASSIGNMENT: A HOMEWORK CHECKLIST

In Class:

   ☐ You have written down the assignment and its deadline.

   ☐ You know what books, materials, and

information you'll need to complete the assignment.

☐ You understand the purpose of the assignment.

☐ You have asked questions about those parts of the assignment you don't understand.

At-Home Checklist:

For textbook reading assignments:

☐ You've read over the headings and subheadings to see how the material is organized.

☐ You have skimmed the material once to get a general idea of what it's about.

☐ You have read everything over a second time more slowly.

☐ You have taken notes on important points as you have read.

☐ You have dated your notes and written down the page numbers so that you will know where to find this review material for a test.

For written exercises and workbook assignments:

☐ You have read over the directions twice.

☐ You have skimmed the whole exercise to see what it's about.

☐ You have completed the easiest examples first just to warm up.

☐ You have worked as hard as possible on the more difficult examples.

☐ You have written down questions to ask the teacher about any examples you couldn't complete.

BOOKING IT: A TEXTBOOK CHECKLIST

☐ Familiarize yourself with the various sections of a textbook (foreword, preface, table of contents, bibliography, index).

☐ Read over the entire table of contents when you first receive your textbook. (Do this periodically, especially before tests, to keep an overview of the course in your mind.)

☐ Survey each chapter as it is assigned —chapter title, main headings, subheadings, and anything else in bold type. (These state the main ideas or guide you to them.)

☐ Skim the questions at the end of each chapter *before* you read the chapter.

☐ Pay special attention to words in heavy type, italics, introductory and concluding sentences and paragraphs. (These are the probable locations of main ideas.)

☐ Take note of visual information — graphs, tables, diagrams.

☐ Outline textbook chapters if you can't underline in your book. (Use the heavy-type headings and subheadings from the chapter for your outline entries. Fill in examples below the headings.)

☐ Answer these questions about assigned chapters:

    ☐ What does the chapter title mean?

    ☐ What do I already know about this subject?

    ☐ What information has my teacher given me about this chapter?

    ☐ What do the headings and subheadings mean?

    ☐ What questions do I have about the chapter?

COUNTDOWN: TEST PREPARATION CHECKLIST

☐ Ask your teacher which materials will be covered on the test.

☐ Find out what kind of test will be given — objective, essay, multiple choice, true-false, etc.

☐ Listen for clues from your teacher during the days or weeks before the test.

☐ Set up a study schedule to prepare for a big test:

    ☐ First, catch up on missing assignments, clear up your notes, fill in blank spots, read over old tests to plan current strategy, talk to people who've been through the course.

☐ Make up study aids (main idea lists, definition sheets, time lines, or outlines) to review.

☐ Do a final sprint the two nights before the test. This step involves: rereading or memorizing underlined material; doing memory work of facts, dates, rules, etc. Reread recently stressed material.

☐ Get a good night's sleep.

PUT TO THE TEST: TEST-TAKING CHECKLIST

☐ Be on time and well equipped for the test.

☐ Listen carefully to your teacher's comments.

☐ Read the directions three times. Skim the whole set of instructions once to get a sense of the requirements. Read them a second time and underline key words. Reread them a third time to fix everything in your mind.

☐ Quickly figure out a schedule for the test. Find a place to write it (scrap paper, corner of the test sheet, reverse side).

☐ Skim all the questions to get a sense of what your teacher is asking and to pick out easiest examples to tackle first.

☐ Read each question three times and underline key words. Here are some of them to look for:

all	always	more	good
every	often	equal	better
most	usually	less	best
many	sometimes	fewer	bad
few	seldom		worse
none	rarely		worst
	never		

☐ Do the easiest examples first. Put a question mark next to those you can't answer but want to go back to.

☐ Go back and answer questions you marked. Put a double mark next to examples you still can't answer.

☐ If you have time left, tackle the double-marked examples.

☐ Guess answers if only right answers are counted.

☐ Double check your answers. Don't change anything without good reason.

☐ Learn from your mistakes. Save all your tests to plan your strategy for future tests and to determine your strengths and weaknesses.

ON THE LINE: AN OUTLINE FORM

Here's the basic format for note-taking outlines or pre-writing outlines. You can skip some steps or add others. (The formal outlining rules state that every main heading must have at least two subheadings to ensure that the main idea is sufficiently broad. If you are outlining strictly for your own use, it isn't necessary to follow these rules exactly. The outline is a set of blueprints, not a commandment.)

TOPIC: _____

I. _____
   A. _____
      1. _____
      2. _____
   B. _____
      1. _____
      2. _____
II. _____
   A. _____
      1. _____
      2. _____
   B. _____
      1. _____
      2. _____
III. _____
   A. _____
      1. _____
      2. _____
   B. _____
      1. _____
      2. _____

PROVING GROUND: A PROOFREADING CHECKLIST

1. Place this checklist side by side with a rough draft of your paper.
2. Read over your paper *once*. Check off items in the "Organization" section of this checklist as you correct the related errors on your paper.
3. Reread your paper a *second* time, checking for errors in the "Grammar and Mechanics" section.
4. Rewrite your draft neatly and clearly into your final copy.

Organization:

☐ My papers focuses on one central topic.
☐ Each paragraph develops an aspect of the central topic.
☐ I have supported each idea with examples and details.

Grammar and Mechanics:

☐ I have indented all paragraphs.
☐ I have used only complete sentences.
☐ Each sentence is capitalized at the beginning.
☐ Each sentence ends with the proper punctuation mark.
☐ All words are spelled correctly to my knowledge.
☐ All verb tenses are consistent throughout the paper.
☐ The paper is neat and readable.

Style:

- [ ] I have used clear and vivid language.
- [ ] I have varied the sentence patterns.
- [ ] I have connected paragraphs with transitional words.
- [ ] I have written a clear concluding paragraph that sums up the topic of the paper.

INDEX